CAMBRIDGE LIBRARY COLLECTION

Books of enduring scholarly value

Medieval History

This series includes pioneering editions of medieval historical accounts by eye-witnesses and contemporaries, collections of source materials such as charters and letters, and works that applied new historiographical methods to the interpretation of the European middle ages. The nineteenth century saw an upsurge of interest in medieval manuscripts, texts and artefacts, and the enthusiastic efforts of scholars and antiquaries made a large body of material available in print for the first time. Although many of the analyses have been superseded, they provide fascinating evidence of the academic practices of their time, while a considerable number of texts have still not been re-edited and are still widely consulted.

The Anonimalle Chronicle 1307 to 1334

This 1991 publication contains the first printed edition of a short continuation of the Anglo-Norman prose *Brut* found in the *Anonimalle Chronicle*. This fourteenth-century chronicle of British history was written at St Mary's Abbey, York, which was a prominent religious centre at the time. Notable for being the most complete example of the text to be found, the continuation here is a valuable source for the wars and political crises of the reign of Edward II and the early reign of Edward III. The manuscript, its contents and value are all discussed in a thorough introduction, while the text is presented with a facing-page translation into English. The work was edited by Wendy Childs, Emeritus Professor of Later Medieval History at Leeds, and John Taylor (1925–2009), former Reader in Medieval History at Leeds.

Cambridge University Press has long been a pioneer in the reissuing of out-of-print titles from its own backlist, producing digital reprints of books that are still sought after by scholars and students but could not be reprinted economically using traditional technology. The Cambridge Library Collection extends this activity to a wider range of books which are still of importance to researchers and professionals, either for the source material they contain, or as landmarks in the history of their academic discipline.

Drawing from the world-renowned collections in the Cambridge University Library and other partner libraries, and guided by the advice of experts in each subject area, Cambridge University Press is using state-of-the-art scanning machines in its own Printing House to capture the content of each book selected for inclusion. The files are processed to give a consistently clear, crisp image, and the books finished to the high quality standard for which the Press is recognised around the world. The latest print-on-demand technology ensures that the books will remain available indefinitely, and that orders for single or multiple copies can quickly be supplied.

The Cambridge Library Collection brings back to life books of enduring scholarly value (including out-of-copyright works originally issued by other publishers) across a wide range of disciplines in the humanities and social sciences and in science and technology.

The Anonimalle Chronicle
1307 to 1334

From Brotherton Collection MS 29

EDITED BY WENDY R. CHILDS
AND JOHN TAYLOR

CAMBRIDGE
UNIVERSITY PRESS

CAMBRIDGE UNIVERSITY PRESS

Cambridge, New York, Melbourne, Madrid, Cape Town,
Singapore, São Paolo, Delhi, Mexico City

Published in the United States of America by Cambridge University Press, New York

www.cambridge.org
Information on this title: www.cambridge.org/9781108061926

© in this compilation Cambridge University Press 2013

This edition first published 1991
This digitally printed version 2013

ISBN 978-1-108-06192-6 Paperback

The Anniversary Reissue of Volumes from the Record Series of the Yorkshire Archaeological Society

To celebrate the 150th anniversary of the foundation of the leading society for the study of the archaeology and history of England's largest historic county, Cambridge University Press has reissued a selection of the most notable of the publications in the Record Series of the Yorkshire Archaeological Society. Founded in 1863, the Society soon established itself as the major publisher in its field, and has remained so ever since. The *Yorkshire Archaeological Journal* has been published annually since 1869, and in 1885 the Society launched the Record Series, a succession of volumes containing transcriptions of diverse original records relating to the history of Yorkshire, edited by numerous distinguished scholars. In 1932 a special division of the Record Series was created which, up to 1965, published a considerable number of early medieval charters relating to Yorkshire. The vast majority of these publications have never been superseded, remaining an important primary source for historical scholarship.

Current volumes in the Record Series are published for the Society by Boydell and Brewer. The Society also publishes parish register transcripts; since 1897, over 180 volumes have appeared in print. In 1974, the Society established a programme to publish calendars of over 650 court rolls of the manor of Wakefield, the originals of which, dating from 1274 to 1925, have been in the safekeeping of the Society's archives since 1943; by the end of 2012, fifteen volumes had appeared. In 2011, the importance of the Wakefield court rolls was formally acknowledged by the UK committee of UNESCO, which entered them on its National Register of the Memory of the World.

The Society possesses a library and archives which constitute a major resource for the study of the county; they are housed in its headquarters, a Georgian villa in Leeds. These facilities, initially provided solely for members, are now available to all researchers. Lists of the full range of the Society's scholarly resources and publications can be found on its website, www.yas.org.uk.

THE ANONIMALLE CHRONICLE
1307 to 1334

Folio 248v from the original manuscript of the Anonimalle Chronicle, reproduced by kind permission of the Brotherton Collection, University of Leeds.

A PDF of the colour image originally positioned here can be downloaded from the web address given on page iv of this book, by clicking on 'Resources Available'.

THE YORKSHIRE
ARCHÆOLOGICAL SOCIETY
FOUNDED 1863   INCORPORATED 1893

RECORD SERIES
VOLUME CXLVII
FOR THE YEAR 1987

THE
ANONIMALLE CHRONICLE
1307 to 1334

From Brotherton Collection MS 29

EDITED BY
WENDY R. CHILDS
AND
JOHN TAYLOR

PRINTED FOR THE SOCIETY
1991

Hon. General Editor
SYLVIA THOMAS

ISBN: 0 902122 59 2

Printed in England by the University Printing Service at
THE UNIVERSITY OF LEEDS

In memory
V. H. G.

Contents

Preface

The discovery of a medieval chronicle is a rare event, and few chronicles of significance for the history of late medieval England have come to light since the publication of the concluding section of the Anonimalle Chronicle in 1927. The Anonimalle Chronicle, which was written at St Mary's Abbey, York, came into the possession of the Ingilby family of Ripley Castle. It remained in their possession until 1920 when the concluding section of the chronicle was identified as a narrative once known to sixteenth-century antiquaries. This section was published by Professor V. H. Galbraith and its account, extending from 1333 to 1381, was immediately recognised as an historical source of first-rate importance particularly by reason of its descriptions of the Good Parliament of 1376, and of the Peasants' Revolt of 1381. During the 1920s the Anonimalle manuscript was purchased by Mr H. L. Bradfer-Lawrence. It was subsequently deposited in the Fitzwilliam Museum, Cambridge, and remained there until its acquisition by the Leeds University Brotherton Collection in 1982. An examination of the manuscript while at Leeds led to the further discovery that in addition to its unique concluding section the narrative contained from 1307 to 1333 the fullest text we possess of the hitherto unpublished short continuation of the French prose *Brut*. The continuation, which is found in the folios immediately preceding the section published by Professor Galbraith, is a valuable chronicle source for the reign of Edward II and for the early years of Edward III. Although parts of the continuation have been known to historians, its wider use and a full appreciation of its value have previously been hampered by the lack of any printed text.

The presence of the Anonimalle manuscript at Leeds offered a unique opportunity to provide a printed text of this narrative. In view of the absence of previous work on the *Brut* continuation it seemed appropriate to publish immediately that part of the Anonimalle manuscript which contains the *Brut* continuation together with a concluding section which appears to have been written at St Mary's itself, and which carried the text to 1334. Thus although other surviving manuscripts of the *Brut* continuation have been examined, and are discussed in the introduction, in order to make the chronicle immediately more widely available no attempt has been made to provide variant readings to the text of the *Brut* continuation found in the Anonimalle manuscript. In a few instances, however, defective parts of the manuscript have been supplied from other manuscripts. It is hoped to provide a full, critical, and comparative textual study of the manuscript tradition of the short *Brut* continuation at a later date.

The authors would like to thank the following for their help in the preparation of the text: the staff of the Brotherton Library, and in particular Mr Christopher Sheppard of the Brotherton Collection; Dr Lynette Muir for her help with the French translation; and Mr Ian Moxon for his very considerable assistance. Our thanks also go to Dr Vanessa Harding for information on London, and to Dr A. Grant and to Professor G. W. S. Barrow for help with the names of the Scots present at the battle of Halidon Hill. What errors remain after this generous help are our own responsibility. In conclusion we would like to thank Mrs Ann Dale and Mrs Margaret Walkington for much patient typing and retyping, especially of the text itself, and Mrs Sylvia Thomas for her most valuable editorial guidance.

The officers of the Yorkshire Archaeological Society wish to join the authors in expressing gratitude to the British Academy and to the Brotherton Library, University of Leeds for generous grants towards the publication of this volume. They also acknowledge the continuing support of the Elisabeth Exwood Memorial Trust for the work of the Record Series.

WRC

JT

List of Abbreviations

Ann. Paul.	*Annales Paulini; Chronicles of the Reigns of Edward I and Edward II*, ed. W. Stubbs, I (Rolls Series, 1882)
BIHR	Bulletin of the Institute of Historical Research
BL	British Library
Brid.	*Bridlington: Gesta Edwardi de Carnarvan Auctore Canonico de Bridlingtoniensi; Chronicles of the Reigns of Edward I and Edward II*, ed. W. Stubbs, II (Rolls Series, 1883)
Brut	*The Brut*, ed. F. W. D. Brie, I (Early English Text Society, 1906)
CCR	*Calendar of Close Rolls*
Croniques de London	*Croniques de London*, ed. G. J. Aungier (Camden Society, 28; 1844)
CUL	Cambridge University Library
EETS	Early English Text Society
EHD	*English Historical Documents*
EHR	*English Historical Review*
Flores	*Flores Historiarum*, ed. H. R. Luard, III (Rolls Series, 1890)
Foedera	*Foedera, Conventiones, Litterae . . .*, T. Rymer (Royal Commission, London, 1816–18)
Guisborough	*Chronicle of Walter of Guisborough*, ed. H. Rothwell (Camden Society, 3rd series, 89; 1957)
'Hemingburgh'	*Chronicon Walteri de Hemingburgh*, ed. H. C. Hamilton (English Historical Society, 1848–9)
Historical Writing	Antonia Gransden, *Historical Writing in England* (2 vols., London, 1974–82)
Knighton	*Chronicon Henrici Knighton*, ed. J. R. Lumby, I (Rolls Series, 1889)
Lanercost	*Chronicon de Lanercost 1201–1346*, ed. J. Stevenson (Bannantyne Club, Edinburgh, 1839)
Le Baker	*Chronicon Galfridi Le Baker de Swynebroke*, ed. E. M. Thompson (Oxford, 1889)
Melsa	*Chronica Monasterii de Melsa*, ed. E. A. Bond, II (Rolls Series, 1867)
Murimuth	*Adae Murimuth Continuatio Chronicarum*, ed. E. M. Thompson (Rolls Series, 1889)
Parl. Writs.	*Parliamentary Writs*, ed. F. Palgrave (London, 1827–34)

Polychronicon	*Polychronicon Ranulphi Higden*, ed. J. R. Lumby, VIII (Rolls Series, 1882)
RS	Rolls Series
Scalacronica	*Scalacronica*, ed. J. Stevenson (Maitland Club, Edinburgh, 1836)
Trokelowe	*Johannis de Trokelowe et Henrici de Blaneforde Chronica et Annales*, ed. H. T. Riley (Rolls Series, 1866)
Vita	*Vita Edwardi Secundi*, ed. N. Denholm-Young (Nelson's Medieval Texts, London, 1957)

Introduction

1. St Mary's and Yorkshire Chronicles

The writing of chronicles in post-Conquest Yorkshire begins in the first half of the twelfth century. At that time the Cistercian settlement was a major influence on chronicle writing. The quality of the Cistercian composition is seen especially in the work of Ailred of Rievaulx whose main historical writings, the *Genealogia Regum Anglorum*, the *Vita Sancti Edwardi Regis et Confessoris*, and the *Relatio de Standardo* comprise an important addition to northern history.[1] In his work Ailred, who looked back to the Old Northumbrian kingdom, conveys some impression of 'a concept of the North' as held by contemporaries. By the thirteenth century, however, the great days of the Cistercian settlement were over. No Yorkshire Cistercian continued the tradition of chronicle writing until in the fourteenth century a number of Cistercian works appear represented by the universal history found at Jervaulx ('John of Brompton'), the domestic history of Meaux written by Abbot Burton, and the two chronicles compiled at Kirkstall Abbey.[2] Neither do many Mendicant chronicles originate in this area although we possess an historical commentary on the Bridlington prophecies by John Erghome, an Austin friar of York, and parts of Franciscan chronicles are also transcribed in Yorkshire sources. What is apparent at the beginning of the fourteenth century is a remarkable tradition of chronicle writing by Austin canons at Guisborough and Bridlington. These chronicles will be considered later, but it should be noted that Augustinian houses were important and wealthy communities, they possessed extensive libraries, and in the person of William of Newburgh, the twelfth-century Austin canon of Newburgh, they could look back on one of the outstanding chroniclers of post-Conquest Yorkshire.[3]

---

[1] Ailred's works are printed in Migne, *Patrologia Latina*, CXCV. The account of the Battle of the Standard is also printed in *Chronicles of Stephen* (RS 1884–9), ed. Howlett, III, 179–99. F. M. Powicke's account of Ailred in *Ailred of Rievaulx and his biographer, Walter Daniel* is still worth consulting, *Bulletin of John Rylands Library*, VII (1922), 310–51, 452–521.

[2] See p. 10.

[3] See pp. 6–9. On William of Newburgh see *Historical Writing*, I, 263–8. Also Rudolf Jahncke, *Ein pragmatischer Geschichtsschreiber des Zwölften Jahrhunderts* (Bonn, 1912).

This gap between the chronicles of the twelfth and those of the late thirteenth and early fourteenth centuries is spanned by the writings of St Mary's, York. Benedictine chronicles, the main strand in the historical writing of medieval England, were never prominent in Yorkshire, and St Mary's, the premier Benedictine foundation in the North, had during the first two centuries of its existence a disappointing chronicle achievement. The main historical output at St Mary's during the period of the thirteenth and early fourteenth centuries consists of a series of annals covering the years from 1258 to 1326. These annals are found now only in a fourteenth-century manuscript, MS Bodley 39. Also in this same manuscript is found a brief account of the foundation of the abbey, and a list of abbots from 1112 to 1258.[4] The St Mary's annals extending from 1258 to 1326 appear to have been compiled in their present form sometime after 1312. It may be that the copyist of the first part of the annals, and the author of the contemporary section after 1312, was a monk who transferred from St Mary's to the daughter house of St Bees, for a distinct interest in St Bees is evident in the latter part of the work. In addition to local information concerning the abbey and its monks, the annals deal with such national events as the Barons' Wars of the thirteenth century and the rebellion of Llewellyn of Wales. In the fourteenth century they contain notices concerning Anglo-Scottish relations and Piers Gaveston. Inspired originally perhaps by Simon Warwick, abbot of St Mary's from 1258 to 1296, they were not used by the author of the Anonimalle Chronicle later.[5]

In addition to the St Mary's annals it is possible that the chronicle of 'Walter of Coventry', probably completed in the late thirteenth century, and found now in MS Corpus Christi College, Cambridge, 175, may have a St Mary's origin.[6] The narrative itself contains no positive evidence of the religious centre in which it was written, although there are Leicester

[4] The list of abbots is printed together with the fuller St Mary's annals in *The Chronicle of St Mary's, York*, ed. H. H. E. Craster and M. E. Thornton (Surtees Society, 148, 1934). The account of the foundation has been printed in *Monasticon Anglicanum* by Sir W. Dugdale (re-edited 1846) III, 544–6.
[5] Leland's notes, sometimes cited as evidence of missing St Mary's chronicles, appear to refer principally to the account of the foundation, and to these annals. *Collectanea* (London, 1774), I, 22.
[6] *Memoriale fratris Walteri de Coventria*, ed W. Stubbs, 2 vols. (RS 1872). See also M. R. James, *A Descriptive Catalogue of the MSS in the Library of Corpus Christi College, Cambridge* (Cambridge, 1912), I, 402–5.

references in the marginalia. The chronicle is mainly compi-lation, the most valuable section of which describes the years between 1002 and 1225. This part of its narrative is taken mainly from accounts such as those of Henry of Huntingdon and Roger Howden. An introductory section known as the *Memoriale* deals with the kings of Britain from Brutus to Edward I, and concludes with a prophecy dating from the reign of Edward I concerning the relations between England and Scotland. From the evidence of this section the chronicle appears to have been completed some time during the latter part of Edward I's reign.

There is convincing evidence that the chronicle was compiled in the diocese of York, and almost certainly within the city itself. Thus in addition to a narrative taken from standard sources the compiler added numerous York references of his own. Again he used among his sources northern accounts including Howden, the north country chronicle found in BL Harleian MS 3860, and the *Lives of the Archbishops of York*. Regarding 'Walter of Coventry' himself almost nothing is known. It is just conceivable that he was a secular clerk attached to the Minster, but from the standard ascription of the *Memoriale* to 'brother Walter of Coventry' it seemed more likely to Stubbs that he was a member of the religious orders, and belonged to the abbey of St Mary's.[7] Writing as he appears to have done in the 1290s, he was possibly introduced into the abbey by Abbot Simon Warwick (1258–96), who may have inspired the first draft of the St Mary's annals. As a native of Coventry Walter originated from an area not too far distant from Warwick. No 'Walter of Coventry' however, is found in the St Mary's records, although during the second half of the thirteenth century there is mention in the St Mary's annals of a Walter of Leicester, 'bonus scholaris in arte dialectica', and of a William of Derby, prior of St Bees.[8] It may be that the Leicester references in the marginalia of the Corpus manuscript point to 'Walter of Leicester' as the possible author. As a follower of Abbot Simon he may well have been encouraged to add to the abbey's modest stock of chronicle writing.

There was, however, no continuous tradition of chronicle writing at St Mary's, nor is there evidence of a scriptorium in

---

[7] See Stubbs's introduction to vol. I.
[8] *Chronicle of St Mary's, York*, p. 131.

the monastery. Neither the St Mary's annals nor 'Walter of Coventry' prepare the way for the Anonimalle Chronicle later. The Anonimalle Chronicle itself is the most famous chronicle to emerge not only from St Mary's, but from the north of England during the fourteenth and fifteenth centuries. The manuscript which contains the chronicle (Brotherton Library MS 29) is described below. Here it may suffice to say that the value of the Anonimalle Chronicle is largely the value of its sources.[9] Thus the chronicle contains the best description of a medieval parliament known to survive, that of the Good Parliament of 1376, as well as an unusually well informed account of the Peasants' Revolt of 1381. Almost certainly both passages derive from London sources, and were the work of an eye-witness, possibly a chancery clerk. Compared with the St Mary's annals and 'Walter of Coventry' earlier, the Anonimalle Chronicle appears to come from an altogether different tradition. This may be explained in part by the close associations which had built up between St Mary's and the central administration during the course of the fourteenth century. By the middle years of that century (a time when the greater part of the Anonimalle Chronicle itself was copied and composed) St Mary's could look back to a period when York had been the second centre of government, and St Mary's itself had been at the hub of national affairs. During the 1330s the English government was based at York, St Mary's had on occasion housed the Chancery,[10] while from the time of Thoresby there was a strong York element present in the Chancery. These associations may well explain the presence in the chronicle of continuations which appear to be the work of chancery clerks.[11] Apart from its links with the Chancery, St Mary's had also a direct involvement with Edward III's Scottish wars, the abbot acting as a kind of 'temporary treasurer' for money raised to finance the English campaign of 1333.[12] This almost certainly explains the interest in Anglo-Scottish affairs evident in the introductory material (fo. 35) as well as in certain

---

[9] On the Anonimalle Chronicle see V. H. Galbraith (ed.), *The Anonimalle Chronicle 1333–81* (Manchester, 1927, repr. 1970); John Taylor, *English Historical Literature in the Fourteenth Century* (Oxford, 1987), chapter 7; *Historical Writing*, II, 110–13, 164–8.

[10] See *English Historical Literature*, pp. 144–5.

[11] See p. 20, n. 63.

[12] Ranald Nicholson, *Edward III and the Scots* (Oxford, 1965), p. 116. For another St Mary's reference in connection with the expedition of 1333 see *The Register of William Melton*, ed. Rosalind Hill (Canterbury and York Society, 1988), III, 120.

parts of the fourteenth-century narrative. A genealogy of the kings of England in the Bodleian Library (Bodleian rolls 3), which once belonged to the abbey, may again have been in the possession of the abbey on account of a St Mary's interest in the English king's claims to overlordship in Scotland.[13]

The surviving books of St Mary's suggest a library of moderate size. The majority of surviving manuscripts were written during the later Middle Ages, and include at least one classical text (Ovid), as well as the works of Boethius, Aquinas, Duns Scotus, and two copies of Richard Rolle.[14] The historical items found there have already been mentioned. Compared with the library of the Austin friary at York which was catalogued in 1377, and which originally comprised some 250 volumes, augmented by John Erghome's private collection of over two hundred items, the St Mary's collection appears to have been a modest affair.[15] Of a library building as such we have no information, although the name of at least one monk, John Graystoke, is mentioned in the fifteenth century as a librarian.[16]

In addition to the texts already mentioned a custumal of St Mary's in MS Bodley 39 gives an account of the duties of the principal officers of the abbey. A consuetudinary of 1390 also survives in MS D.27 of St John's College, Cambridge, which conveys some impression of the religious routine within the monastery.[17] This consisted of the performance of the Divine Office, the obits, and the services owed to other monasteries. From this and other evidence we can see that by the fourteenth century St Mary's was one of the most prestigious religious institutions in the North. It was a 'pedigree community' which could look back upon a long history. Its abbots such as William Marrays were important figures in the meetings of Benedictine general chapters. It is not surprising therefore that at the peak of its influence, and at an important phase in the history of medieval York, the abbey produced in the Anonimalle Chronicle an historical narrative of quite unusual interest.

---

[13] N. Ker, *Medieval Libraries of Great Britain* (Royal Historical Society, 1964), p. 217.
[14] Ibid.
[15] On Erghome see *infra*. For a recent account of Erghome's library see K. W. Humphreys, 'The Library of John Erghome, and Personal Libraries in Fourteenth Century England', *A Medieval Miscellany in Honour of Professor John Le Patourel* (Proceedings of the Leeds Philosophical and Literary Society 18, 2, 1982), pp. 106–23.
[16] See pp. 21–2.
[17] M. R. James *A Descriptive Catalogue of the MSS in the Library of St John's College, Cambridge* (Cambridge, 1913), pp. 135–7.

Because of the existence of the Anonimalle Chronicle St Mary's must be regarded as the premier centre of chronicle writing in Yorkshire during the second half of the fourteenth century. During the reigns of Edward I and Edward II, however, the houses of Austin canons at Guisborough and Bridlington as mentioned above had produced important narratives which are of value for both national and northern events, and which should be briefly mentioned. At the Augustinian priory of Guisborough Walter of Guisborough wrote a chronicle which began with the Norman Conquest and extended to 1305.[18] His chronicle, which appears to have circulated in a number of copies, survives in some ten manuscripts. It was one source for Henry Knighton's chronicle at Leicester, while portions of the text were also worked into the Osney-Abingdon compilations in the south later. Walter of Guisborough is traditionally the great chronicler of Edward I's later years. Recent work suggests, however, that his account is not reliable as a general guide to events during that reign.[19] For northern history Guisborough's narrative is more firmly based, and particularly for its description of Anglo-Scottish affairs. Of particular interest in this section of the chronicle is the relationship between Guisborough's narrative and other northern accounts. Thus there is a relationship between Guisborough's description of Anglo-Scottish affairs under Edward I, and the account contained in another northern chronicle (BL MS Harleian 3860). Joseph Stevenson, who printed a part of the Harleian chronicle in *Wallace Papers*, thought that the chronicle was Guisborough's source for these passages.[20] It may be, however, that the two narratives were indebted to a common source which is now missing. It is perhaps worth noting that the chronicle of Thomas of Castleford, which survives in a single manuscript at Göttingen, and which contains several entries on Anglo-Scottish history, also has similarities with the Harleian chronicle.[21] Again 'Walter of Coventry' in the first part of his chronicle used an account similar to the opening of the Harleian narrative. There was

---

[18] Walter of Guisborough, *Chronicle*, ed. H. Rothwell (Camden Society, 89, 1957); *Historical Writing*, I, 470–6.
[19] Guisborough, *Chronicle*, p. xxix.
[20] *Wallace Papers* (Maitland Club, 1841). See Guisborough, *Chronicle*, p. xxvii.
[21] See p. 11.

clearly therefore some form of borrowing between the northern chronicles of this period.

Walter of Guisborough is the author of the only chronicle known to survive from that house. It has been suggested that parts of a missing Guisborough chronicle may lie behind the fourteenth-century part of the Anonimalle account.[22] However, although references to Guisborough are found in the Anonimalle text, they are neither so numerous nor so unusual as to constitute irrefutable evidence of this hypothesis. A different problem concerns the continuations of the Guisborough chronicle. It is probable that the continuation from 1305 to 1312 was the work of a Durham scribe.[23] A further continuation, covering the years from 1327 to 1347, known traditionally as 'the continuation of Hemingburgh', was printed by Hamilton in an early edition of Guisborough's chronicle at a time when the author of that chronicle passed under the name of 'Walter of Hemingburgh'.[24] This continuation is found together with the full text of Guisborough only in one sixteenth-century transcript (Trinity College Cambridge MS R.5.10). It has no intrinsic connection with the chronicle of Walter of Guisborough ('Hemingburgh'), and appears to be a version of the text of the *Historia Aurea* covering the years from 1327 to 1347.[25] The *Historia Aurea* itself was a northern compilation, possibly written by John of Wheteley, who was vicar of Tynemouth during the 1350s and 1360s. The fourteenth-century part of his massive compilation was often used as a source by contemporary chroniclers. The account of the *Historia Aurea* for these years survives, however, in more than one version. The text printed by Hamilton as 'the continuation of Hemingburgh' differs from other copies in a number of instances, notably by its inclusion of the battle formations at Halidon Hill. It seems likely therefore that the scribe of this particular version of the *Historia Aurea* ('the continuation of Hemingburgh') had access to some official list, similar but not identical to the one transcribed in the Anonimalle account.[26]

---

[22] J. G. Edwards's review of Galbraith's edition in *EHR* 43 (1928), 103–9.
[23] See Guisborough, *Chronicle*, p. xxi.
[24] Guisborough, *Chronicle*, pp. xxiv seq.
[25] Ibid. pp. xxiii–xxiv.
[26] See Appendix 3. On the *Historia Aurea* and the continuation of 'Hemingburgh' see V. H. Galbraith, 'Sources of the St Albans Chronicle', *Essays in History Presented to R. L. Poole*, ed. H. W. C Davis (Oxford, 1927), pp. 379–98.

Compared with Guisborough, the Austin house at Bridlington has a better recorded tradition of chronicle writing. At Bridlington the priory appears to have been a notable centre of historical studies during the early part of the fourteenth century, and Bridlington chronicles were among those selected by the king's commissioners when Edward I made his historical claim to the overlordship of Scotland.[27] At this house the best known of all writers is undoubtedly Peter Langtoft, a canon of Bridlington who as his name suggests almost certainly came from Langtoft, close to Bridlington, in the East Riding of Yorkshire.[28] Langtoft appears to have been the house's 'man of business', acting at times as prior's attorney or on behalf of the chapter in Yorkshire. In his business acumen Langtoft was typical of a number of fourteenth-century writers. His chronicle, which is in rhyming French, draws on Geoffrey of Monmouth's romantic history for its opening, but is chiefly valuable for its account of Edward I's reign. Like other Yorkshire writers Langtoft concerned himself with the Anglo-Scottish wars, and this part of his chronicle was one source of the Anonimalle account. Langtoft's description of Edward I's campaigns is noteworthy for its violent anti-Scottish bias, which contrasts markedly with the more moderate tone adopted by Walter of Guisborough. The interest of this account as one indication of contemporary feeling is increased by the author's inclusion in his work of a number of popular songs.[29] These songs were almost certainly composed in English but on occasion Langtoft appears to have translated the English version into French. Langtoft's chronicle was clearly intended for a general audience of both clergy and laity, and his work represents the best example we have of the 'popularizing' of history in Yorkshire at this time.

Langtoft's account was not the only chronicle to be composed at Bridlington during the later Middle Ages. In the first half of the fourteenth century an unknown canon of that house wrote in Latin a first-rate account of English history from 1307 to 1339 (with a number of additional entries between 1340 and

[27] *Documents and Records Illustrating the History of Scotland*, ed. F. Palgrave (Record Commission, 1837), pp. 60–7.

[28] *Pierre de Langtoft, Chronicle*, ed. T. Wright, 2 vols (RS 1866–8). A new edition of the final part of this chronicle is found in *Pierre de Langtoft, Le Règne d'Édouard 1er*, édition critique par Jean Claude Thiolier C.E.L.I.M.A. (Université de Paris 12, 1989). See also M. D. Legge, *Anglo-Norman in the Cloisters* (Edinburgh, 1950), pp. 70–4; *Historical Writing*, I, 476–86.

[29] Langtoft, *Chronicle*, II, 234–6.

1377).[30] This account includes much that is of interest for northern history including a description of the campaign of 1333. The narrative, known as the *Gesta Edwardi de Carnarvan*, appears to be based upon an earlier text which extended as far as 1339. The quality of this Bridlington account is enhanced by the inclusion in its text of a number of historical documents drawn from the collection at Bridlington and known as the *Incidentia Chronicorum*. For the 1320s and 1330s the Bridlington chronicle has entries in common with the Anonimalle narrative. This relationship is considered elsewhere, but it is possible that the two chronicles used a common source, namely a set of annals which circulated in the York diocese at the time.[31]

In addition to Langtoft's chronicle and the *Gesta Edwardi de Carnarvan* it seems likely that a collection of political prophecies, known as the Bridlington prophecies, written in Latin, whose main purpose was criticism of what their author saw as the ineffective conduct of the war with France, were also composed at Bridlington during the middle years of the century.[32] Although there is much that is unclear about these prophecies, including their ascription to John of Bridlington, the saintly fourteenth-century prior of the house, it seems probable that they were composed there and did not originate outside the priory. A strong presumption for a Bridlington origin can be deduced from the fact that the prophecies are quoted in the Bridlington account, the *Gesta Edwardi de Carnarvan*. It seems unlikely they would have been included in that source had they been a fabrication composed elsewhere.

To these prophecies, which circulated widely during the second half of the fourteenth century, John Erghome, the well-known Austin friar of York, added an historical commentary which drew on sources such as the *Polychronicon* of Ranulf Higden. John Erghome's quasi-historical commentary almost certainly derives from a concern with contemporary affairs evident in literate circles in York during the 1360s. There was at this time in York, as elsewhere, intense interest in the campaigns in France, and dissatisfaction with the terms of the Treaty of Bretigny. An implicit criticism of the conduct of the

---

[30] The *Gesta Edwardi de Carnarvan* is printed in *Chronicles of the Reigns of Edward I and II*, ed. W. Stubbs (RS 1882–3) II, 25–151; *Historical Writing*, II, 9–11, 113–15.

[31] See pp. 63–4. There may be early Bridlington annals which are now missing; Guisborough, *Chronicle*, p. xxvi.

[32] The prophecies were edited by T. Wright in *Political Poems and Songs* (RS 1859), I, 123–215. See the comments of and literature quoted in *English Historical Literature*, pp. 239–42.

war with France is one principal feature of Erghome's work. This phase of the Hundred Years War is also reflected in the latter part of the Anonimalle account which describes in some detail the campaigns of the 1360s and 1370s, campaigns in which northern magnates were actively involved.[33]

At the end of the fourteenth century, and at a time when chronicle writing at St Mary's and at the Austin houses had virtually ceased, the chronicle gap was filled by Cistercian accounts from Meaux and Kirkstall. At Meaux Abbot Burton wrote what is one of the most substantial domestic accounts of a Cistercian monastery known to survive.[34] Burton was undoubtedly aided in his work by the fact that he had been for a time in charge of the abbey's finances, and knew at first hand something of the problems of running a Cistercian community.[35] At Kirkstall the long Kirkstall chronicle gives an account of the French campaigns of the middle years of the century. This account which borrows extensively from the Bridlington prophecies is far less detailed and well-informed than the Anonimalle narrative.[36] By way of contrast the short Kirkstall chronicle provides a detailed description of the final years of Richard II's reign which may draw upon missing sources including a lost Franciscan narrative.[37]

The Yorkshire chronicles which have been described reveal that there existed some substantial borrowing between these northern accounts. Evident also in these writings is a general concern with the Scottish and French wars. What they do not reveal, however, is a common tradition of chronicle writing. Most are occasional productions. They do not originate from a well-established background of chronicle production in the North. Again while most Yorkshire chronicles were written in Latin, the traditional language of the Church, two of the outstanding narratives of the fourteenth century, the Anonimalle Chronicle and Langtoft's account, were written in French. In this century only one Yorkshire chronicle, that of Thomas of Castleford, was originally composed in English.

[33] See J. Taylor, 'Higden and Erghome: two fourteenth-century scholars' in *Économies et Sociétés au Moyen Age: Mélanges offerts à Edouard Perroy* (Publications de la Sorbonne, série Etudes V, Paris, 1973), pp. 644–9; *Anonimalle Chronicle*, pp. 65, 176n.

[34] *Chronica Monasterii de Melsa*, ed. E. Bond (RS 1866–8) 3 vols; *Historical Writing*, II, 355–71 gives a full account of this chronicle.

[35] On Burton's financial expertise see Antonia Gransden, 'Antiquarian Studies in Fifteenth-Century England' (*Antiquaries Journal*, 60, 1, 1980), 75–97.

[36] *The Kirkstall Abbey Chronicles*, ed. J. Taylor (Thoresby Society, 42, 1952), pp. 86–97.

[37] Ibid. pp. 52–85, 98–129.

Of Thomas of Castleford himself we know almost nothing except that he was probably a secular clerk, that he came from Pontefract, and that he compiled what appears to be the earliest Yorkshire chronicle written in the English language.[38] The chronicle (MS Göttingen Hist. 740) begins like the Anonimalle account with the *Brut* history. It draws on Langtoft for some of its later narrative. Its account of the reigns of Edward I and Edward II, where the author goes into some detail on Anglo-Scottish affairs, is mostly original, although even here the chronicle has some similarities with BL MS Harleian 3860. The account which ends at 1327 reflects a concern with Anglo-Scottish relations explained by Yorkshire's position as a forward base against the Scots. The fact that the chronicle was written in English may perhaps be seen as part of a gradual movement towards the English vernacular, evident later in Robert Mannyng of Bourne's English translation of Langtoft. The extent to which chronicles in this region, written in English and French, were expressly designed for a lay audience is perhaps uncertain. Langtoft's rhyming chronicle composed in French was undoubtedly intended for a lay as well as an ecclesiastical audience. Thomas of Castleford may well have had a lay audience in mind. Nonetheless the most important historical narrative written in the north of England, the Anonimalle Chronicle which was composed in French, was almost certainly written with no outside audience in mind, and appears to have been virtually unknown outside St Mary's itself.

---

[38] On Thomas of Castleford see *English Historical Literature*, pp. 152–3. A study of the chronicle is found in M. L. Perrin, *Über Thomas Castelfords Chronik* (Boston, 1890).

2. The Brotherton manuscript and its contents

The manuscript

The text printed in this volume is part of Brotherton Collection MS 29 (Anonimalle Chronicle). This MS, which was written in the second half of the fourteenth century at St Mary's Abbey, York, may be divided into the following sections:

1. fos. 1–35v. A number of miscellaneous items written in French and Latin.

2. fos. 36–248v. A type of *Brut* chronicle written in French.

3. fos. 248v–271. The most complete text of the short continuation of the French prose *Brut* chronicle (1307–33).

4. fos. 271–303v. A further continuation in French covering the years 1333 to 1369 and using a missing Franciscan source of the Lanercost chronicle as well as official documents and newsletters.

5. fos. 304–353v. A continuation in French covering the years 1369 to 1381 using London sources. This continuation contains the descriptions of the Good Parliament (1376) and the Peasants' Revolt (1381).

Items 4 and 5 were printed by V. H. Galbraith as *The Anonimalle Chronicle 1333–1381* (Manchester, 1927, reprinted 1970). For a fuller description of the contents of the whole manuscript see pp. xxiii–xxiv of that edition, and *English Historical Literature*, pp. 133–53. The probability that the entire manuscript was copied at St Mary's Abbey, York, is deduced from the evidence of the handwriting. The *Brut* chronicle (fos. 36–248v) is, for example, written in a script which has been described as similar to that of the two St Mary's cartularies preserved in York Minster library.[39] There is again a similarity of script between the short continuation of the *Brut* (fos. 248v–271) and that of the further continuations (fos. 271–353v), which were almost certainly composed at York.[40]

[39] See *Anonimalle Chronicle*, p. xx.
[40] For an examination of this section of the chronicle see *English Historical Literature*, pp. 139–41.

The manuscript has the appearance of having been written over a number of years. The main work of copying the text as far as fo. 271 (1333) was probably done during the middle years of the century, for at fo. 270v there is a reference, 'come vous orrez apres', to William Montagu's being made earl of Salisbury, which happened in 1337 as is duly noted in the subsequent section (fo. 276), which seems to have been already in preparation when the earlier part was being written.[41] Fos. 271–303v, covering the period 1333–69, appear to be the work of a scribe who was working in the 1350s and 1360s. This part of the manuscript was probably written almost contemporaneously with the events which it describes.[42] The final section of the manuscript (fos. 304–353v), covering the years 1369 to 1381, may have been added at a later stage.[43]

The opening folios of the manuscript (fos. 1–35v) contain a number of items which help to confirm the manuscript's provenance, and the dates of composition of its component parts. Thus there is a list of the abbots of St Mary's (fo. 29v) as well as a list of the churches in the gift of St Mary's, York (fos. 34–35). In the list of abbots the final name is that of William Marrays/eys, elected in 1359, whose death in 1382 has been added in a later hand. This list not only suggests a St Mary's provenance, but also the possibility that the main work of copying was done before 1382. Other items in these opening folios, including a genealogical table showing Edward III's claim to the French throne and a prayer in verse for the victory of the English king, appear to refer to the opening stages of the Hundred Years War.[44] Certain items have a direct bearing on the *Brut* chronicle (fos. 36–248v) and on its short continuation. Transcribed in the opening section, for example, is a form of the Anglo-Norman poem, *Des Grantz Geanz* (fos. 23–26), which traditionally formed the preface to the *Brut*.[45] Also found in this early section is a short Latin chronicle (fos. 26v–29), beginning in 1307, which concentrates its narrative principally on the reign of Edward II. Passages from this Latin chronicle are translated in the text of the short continuation.

---

[41] William Montagu was made earl of Salisbury in 1337, see *Anonimalle Chronicle*, p. 9.
[42] The evidence for this is set out in *English Historical Literature*, pp. 139–41.
[43] Ibid. pp. 141–3.
[44] Fos. 2v, 3v, 4v. The authors owe this information to Dr Ruth Dean.
[45] For a study of the manuscript tradition of this opening see *Des Grantz Geanz*, ed. G. E. Brereton (Medium Aevum Monographs, II, Oxford, 1937).

The history of the manuscript subsequent to its compilation in the fourteenth century is of some interest. It was undoubtedly in the possession of St Mary's during the later Middle Ages. There is no evidence that it was known outside that house. At some stage during the sixteenth century, however, the manuscript found its way to London, possibly through a member of the Rudstone family, for what could be the name 'John Rudstone' appears on the first folio. A member of this family, Sir John Rudstone, was Lord Mayor of London in 1528–29, and his family may have had connections with the family of John Stow, the London antiquary.[46] What is certain is that the manuscript, while it was in London, came to the attention of John Stow and his contemporary and fellow antiquary, Francis Thynne. That John Stow knew the manuscript is clear from the fact that notes in his hand occur at fos. 287v, 300v and 316r and v, and that he cited the chronicle in his *Annales*, and *Survey of London*. From the references in his writings Stow appears to have seen the manuscript between 1592 and 1598.[47] Also during the 1590s Thynne made a transcript of that final part of the manuscript which relates to the Peasants' Revolt of 1381. This transcript he described as 'out of an anominalle cronicle belonginge to the abbey of St Maries in Yorke'. V. H. Galbraith, who edited and published the final portion of the manuscript, supposed that Thynne had meant to write 'anonimalle', a synonym for 'anonymous'. Galbraith deliberately used Thynne's description of the whole manuscript as the title for that section of it (fos. 271–353), which he edited in order (i) to suggest the connection of his edition with the Peasants' Rising section (fos. 340v–351) transcribed by Thynne (ed. G. M. Trevelyan, *EHR* 13 (1898), 509–22), and (ii) to associate permanently with the chronicle the names of Thynne and Stow, who both appreciated it and used it. We may, however, allow the title 'Anonimalle Chronicle' to apply to the entire manuscript comprising the main *Brut* chronicle (fos. 36–248v) together with its continuations. In the seventeenth century William Clapham, who had family connections with the Ingilbys at Ripley, caused

---

[46] Sir Edward Rudstone was buried in the church where Stow's ancestors were buried. C. E. Wright, *Fontes Harleiana* (London, 1972); J. Stow, *Survey of London*, ed. C. L. Kingsford (Oxford, 1908), I, 197–8.

[47] The manuscript is not mentioned in the first edition of Stow's *Annales* in 1592, but is mentioned in his *Survey of London* (1598).

the manuscript to be returned to Yorkshire. A note at fo. 281v says 'William Clapham owithe this booke and boight yt at london at mychalemesse laste paste and sent yt downe by Jhon Longe [sic] the carier'. The manuscript remained in the possession of the Ingilby family until the 1920s when it was bought at auction by Mr Bradfer-Lawrence. It was purchased by the University of Leeds for the Brotherton Collection in 1982.

The chronicle

The section of Brotherton Collection MS 29 printed in the present volume from fos. 248v–271, and preserving, as stated, the most complete text of the short continuation of the French prose *Brut* chronicle is preceded in the manuscript (fos. 36–248v) by a type of *Brut* chronicle. The *Brut* chronicle in our manuscript, however, is not a characteristic one. The typical *Brut* chronicle was a French prose narrative written by an unknown author or authors sometime during the reign of Edward I.[48] Its text originally concluded in 1307 but was subsequently continued to 1333. During the middle years of the fourteenth century this French narrative was translated into English, and the French tradition of the prose *Brut* came to an almost complete end. In the course of the fourteenth and fifteenth centuries a number of further continuations were added to the texts of the English version which ultimately carried the English narrative down the the 1470s.[49] Written for no one patron, but addressed initially to an audience of magnates and gentry, the *Brut* chronicle, particularly through the medium of its English version, became the most popular chronicle of late medieval England.

Although the French text of the prose *Brut* was overshadowed and superseded by its English translation, original French texts survive describing events down to 1333. This original French narrative contains the genesis of what was to become the main

---

[48] For a description of the prose *Brut* and its fourteenth-century continuations see *English Historical Literature*, pp. 110–32. The prose *Brut* survives in over two hundred manuscripts, fifty or so in the original French, at least 166 in English, and 15 in Latin. These figures are taken from L. M. Matheson, 'The Middle English Prose *Brut*. A Location List of the Manuscripts and Early Printed Editions' (*Analytical and Enumerative Bibliography*, 3, 1979–80), 255–66. This list supersedes that of F. W. D. Brie, *Geschichte und Quellen der mittelenglischen Prosachronik, 'The Brut of England' oder 'The Chronicles of England'* (Marburg, 1905; repr. 1960).

[49] For an account of the *Brut* in the fifteenth century see C. L. Kingsford, *English Historical Literature in the Fifteenth Century* (Oxford, 1913), pp. 113–39; *Historical Writing*, II, 220–27.

national history produced in England during the later Middle Ages, and it repays careful study. The early part of the French *Brut* chronicle consisted of one or other of several adaptations of Geoffrey of Monmouth's *Historia Regum Britanniae*. The essence of its account originating in Geoffrey of Monmouth was the attribution of the historical origins of Britain to Brutus, the great-grandson of Aeneas, who after many wanderings arrived in Britain to become the first king of the island.[50] After a description of the various mythical rulers who succeeded Brutus, the French prose *Brut* moved to an account of Arthur. According to its narrative Arthur, after conquering England, Scotland and France, 'though without leaving the faintest trace of achievement in the annals or literature of any nation', was ultimately betrayed by his nephew, Mordred.[51] In the *Brut* narrative the legendary history closed with the death of Cadwallader, where Geoffrey's own history had ended. After this came a section covering the time of the early Saxon kings to the death of Edward the Confessor. This derived from a version of Wace's *Brut*, a twelfth-century verse chronicle based in its early section on Geoffrey's compilation. This in turn was followed by a section extending from the reign of William the Conqueror to the death of Henry III. This section used the Cistercian compilation known as the *Annals of Waverley*.[52] A final section described the reign of Edward I (1272–1307) and for this period drew upon the rhyming chronicle of Peter Langtoft.[53]

The prose *Brut* survives in two main versions, traditionally described as the long and the short versions. As far as 1307 both versions use common sources, and preserve what is basically a standard text though with slight variations. The period after 1307 extending to *c.* 1333 was treated by two distinct continuations, a long continuation and a short continuation, attached respectively to the long and the short versions of the prose *Brut*. During the middle years of the fourteenth century the long version of the *Brut* together with

---

[50] Among innumerable studies of this British history should be noted J. S. P. Tatlock, *The Legendary History of Britain* (California, 1950); L. T. D. Kendrick, *British Antiquity* (London, 1950); and L. Keeler, *Geoffrey of Monmouth and the Late Latin Chroniclers 1300–1500* (University of California Press, 1946).

[51] See J. Gairdner, *Early Chronicles of Europe, England* (1879), p. 161, and the comments of Rosemary Morris, *The Character of King Arthur in Medieval Literature* (Brewer, 1982), p. 6.

[52] Brie, *Geschichte und Quellen*, p. 43.

[53] Ibid. p. 44.

its continuation (the long continuation) was translated into English. This English translation was printed in the early years of the present century by the Early English Text Society and, through the medium of that edition, the English text of the long continuation became widely known.[54] By contrast the short continuation, which was attached to the shorter version of the *Brut*, was never translated into English, and its French text has never been printed. Yet as an historical source it is if anything of greater value than the better-known long continuation.

The relationship of the *Brut* chronicle constituting fos. 36–248v of the Brotherton manuscript to the family of *Brut* chronicles cannot yet be established with certainty.[55] Although described by Galbraith as 'the most rare and most elaborate of the French *Brut* chronicles', it is not, as has already been stated above, a characteristic French *Brut*. The narrative, which extends from the time of Brutus to 1307, draws on a variety of sources including Geoffrey of Monmouth, Henry of Huntington, Florence of Worcester, William of Malmesbury and William of Newburgh. Its account shows an interest in ecclesiastical history with entries relating to the Canterbury–York dispute (fos. 149, 175v) and to the archbishops of York (fos. 144v, 157v, 159, 163v, 166–172). This interest and the northern references which it contains serve to distinguish its account from that of the standard text of the prose *Brut*. Another feature which serves to set the Brotherton *Brut* chronicle apart from most others concerns its use of Merlin prophecies. In the prose *Brut* such prophecies, often placed at the conclusion of a reign and forming a type of summary, are a frequent element. They appear also in the long continuation of the *Brut*, though they are not present in the further English continuations extending beyond the reign of Edward II. By contrast neither the Brotherton *Brut* chronicle (fos. 36–248v), nor the short continuation which follows it in the manuscript (fos. 248v–271), employ this device. Merlin and Gildas prophecies are, however, assembled on the opening folios of the manuscript (fos. 10v–19).[56]

---

[54] The English translation is printed in *The Brut or Chronicles of England*, ed. F. W. D. Brie (Early English Text Society, cxxxi, cxxxvi, 1906, 1908; two vols. reprinted 1960), 2, 205–86.

[55] There are innumerable French histories about the kings of England which are known as *Bruts*. See D. B. Tyson, 'An Early French Prose History of the Kings of England' (*Romania*, 96, 1975), 1–26.

[56] There is one Merlin prophecy in Latin at fo. 170v.

The Brotherton *Brut* chronicle, though distinct from the typical French *Brut*, was evidently considered sufficiently close to the *Brut* tradition to be furnished, among the miscellaneous items in the opening folios of the Brotherton manuscript, with the traditional preface to the *Brut* in the form of the Anglo-Norman poem, *Des Grantz Geanz*, and to be provided for the period after 1307, where its narrative concluded, with one of the two standard *Brut* continuations, the text of which is the main subject of the present edition (see below). Texts generally similar to that of the Brotherton *Brut* chronicle (fos. 36–248v) are found in two manuscripts, namely BL MS Royal 20 A XVIII, and BL MS Add. 10622 (which ends incomplete in 1181). These texts, which contain some variations from that of the Brotherton manuscript, may represent attempts to produce a form of *Brut* history fashioned for an ecclesiastical audience, but if that was so they did not achieve any notable success. The *Brut* chronicle in BL MS Royal 20 A XVIII is distinguished from the Brotherton *Brut* chronicle by being followed by the long rather than the short continuation. This version of the long continuation contains interesting variations, and includes a concluding section in which Edward II was rumoured to be still alive. The long continuation in the Royal manuscript is also followed by the prophecies of Merlin, numbered as chapters to fit in at the end of each reign (fos. 336–343v).

The short continuation

Fos. 248v–271 of the Brotherton manuscript are our immediate concern, containing as they do the fullest text we possess of the short continuation of the prose *Brut*. This is one of several surviving texts of the short continuation, few of which are exactly identical, but all having certain features in common. The short continuations are factual and annalistic accounts of contemporary history, different in style both from the prose *Brut* and from other *Brut* continuations. They employ none of the stylistic features of the prose *Brut* such as the use of Merlin prophecies, and the inclusion of anecdotal narrative and direct speech. They have no chapter headings in the manner of the *Brut*. Like the majority of contemporary chronicles the short continuations are sympathetic to Thomas of Lancaster, whom they uniformly portray in a favourable light.[57] They are distinguished also by their forthright denunciation of the Despensers.[58]

The evidence that the Brotherton text of the short continuation, like other items in the Brotherton manuscript, was copied at St Mary's during the middle years of the fourteenth century has already been cited.[59] The history of its composition is, however, more complex. There is some evidence to suggest that the Brotherton text of the short continuation existed in some form before it came to St Mary's. Alone among the copies of the continuation it contains a number of brief passages which refer to the Franciscan order, and to the city of York. There is for example mention of a Franciscan who was made cardinal in 1312, of the damage done to the house of the Greyfriars at York by floods in 1315, and of trouble with the Spiritual Franciscans in 1327.[60] These Franciscan passages appear to be interpolations in a text which came into the possession of St Mary's. It is difficult to see why a copyist at St Mary's would have introduced the Franciscan passages, yet added no information with respect to his own community. The evidence of these passages suggests therefore the possibility of an earlier Franciscan involvement with the text.

A number of what appear to be interpolations may have been added at St Mary's itself. These include the account of Nicholas Fleming, mayor of York, which is not found in this complete form in any other text of the continuation.[61] Other passages which may have been added at St Mary's include a note on Thomas of Lancaster's burial in the priory church at Pontefract, and the burial also of certain of his principal supporters.[62] The notices on episcopal elections were probably introduced at St Mary's, as well as many of the year dates. Apart from these additions a northern interest is evident in the Edward III section of the continuation with its detailed account of the Anglo-Scottish campaigns of 1332 and 1333. So exact is the detail, including the mention of the occupants of peels, that

---

[57] See pp. 102–8.
[58] See p. 92.
[59] See p. 12.
[60] Fos. 250, 250v, 262v.
[61] See p. 98. The account of Nicholas Fleming occurs in the description of the battle of Myton-on-Swale in 1319, Anonimalle MS fo. 253. He is briefly mentioned in certain Brut continuations such as Bodleian Library MS Douce 128.
[62] See p. 108.

only a writer based in the north, possibly at York, could have written the latter part of the continuation. By way of contrast the early part of the continuation has an undoubted London origin, revealing an intimate knowledge of London history. In view of this difference it seems likely that the continuation was begun in London and then completed at York during the 1330s. The author of this particular continuation may have been a clerk attached to the central administration, possibly the Exchequer, who travelled to York when the administration moved there for a period during the 1330s.[63] This might explain his knowledge of London affairs during the 1320s, and his later concentration upon northern campaigns. It may also explain why the fullest version of the short continuation is found at York, if that was the city where the narrative was completed. Copies of the continuation probably circulated in the city, and one may have been in the possession of the York Greyfriars before passing to St Mary's.

The Brotherton text of the short continuation is not the only surviving copy of that continuation, nor was it the only one in the possession of St Mary's Abbey. The short continuation survives in a number of copies, all of which appear to contain abbreviated or incomplete versions of the fullest text found in the Brotherton manuscript. Thus Cambridge UL MS Gg. 1. 15 and Dublin, Trinity College MS 500 contain slightly shortened versions of the text while BL MS Domitian A. X offers an even shorter text. Certain surviving texts of the short continuation survive only in fragmentary form.[64] Some manuscripts, for example the three fifteenth-century manu-scripts (BL MS Harleian 200, Cambridge Trinity College MS R. 5. 32 and Bodleian MS Douce 128) in which the text of the short continuation is followed by Avesbury's chronicle, contain individualistic versions of some events, e.g. a passage on the

---

[63] This Exchequer suggestion relates to the authorship of the short continuation. The author of the long continuation may have been attached to some writing office close to the Chancery. In the short continuation the author's interest in government supplies is seen perhaps in his detailed account of the movement of siege engines from Northampton and Bamburgh in 1319; see p. 96. The chancery settled in York from 1332 until the end of 1336 with occasional moves to London and to the Midlands. The Exchequer and the Common Bench were also at York in the 1330s; T. F. Tout, *Chapters in the Administrative History of Medieval England* (Manchester, 1923–35), III, 57–9.

[64] BL MS Add. 18462, a fifteenth-century copy which belonged once to Sir Simonds d'Ewes, contains two sides of writing (fos. 204–204v). BL MS Cotton Julius A. VI, includes a fragment of the short continuation of the *Brut* (fos. 51–53v). Almost all the material in these versions is found in the Anonimalle text with the exception of a brief account of the siege of Haddington. See Appendix 4 for a provisional list of these manuscripts.

siege of La Réole, and a passage excusing Queen Isabella for Stapledon's murder. Again Bodleian MS Lyell 17, Lambeth MS 504, and Trinity College Dublin 500 mention the siege of Haddington which is not referred to in the majority of the manuscripts.

In view of the different versions of the short continuation surviving in several manuscripts, it is difficult to establish precisely the point at which the original short continuation ended. A number of versions end at various points in the middle of the 1320s.[65] Others such as the College of Arms MS Arundel 31 end early in Edward III's reign. The versions which precede Avesbury's chronicle end in 1332. MS Lyell 17, MS Lambeth 504, and Trinity College, Dublin 500 among others conclude in 1333 with the siege of Haddington. The version in the Brotherton manuscript appears to end after an account of the battle of Halidon Hill in 1333. Nonetheless the description of this battle appears to be peculiar to the Brotherton version. It is probable therefore that this part of the narrative was composed at St Mary's, and was not part of the original continuation.[66] After the description of the battle the Brotherton version includes also a number of entries on episcopal or archiepiscopal appointments in 1334 in addition to an account of Balliol's homage to Edward III. This version of the continuation may therefore have been further extended to 1334 in the form of a number of brief entries. From its emphasis on the events of 1332 and 1333 it is likely that its original concluding section was written close to these final events, possibly during the middle 1330s, and before the central administration had returned to London.

During the fifteenth century St Mary's Abbey acquired a second manuscript containing the *Brut* continuation, now Bodleian Library MS Lyell 17. A note in the Lyell manuscript, 'De perquisicione Joh. de Graystok liberar.', states that this copy was acquired by John de Graystoke. Graystoke was probably a conventual librarian at St Mary's during the fifteenth century, for his name appears in a number of books belonging

[65] CUL MS Gg. 1. 15 ends in 1326 (but folio displaced) and BL MS Add. 35113 in 1324. It is hoped to publish a fuller account of these continuations at a later date. See M. D. Legge and G. M. Brereton, 'The French Prose Brut, three unlisted MSS' (*Medium Aevum*, 7, 1938), p. 116, n. 7.

[66] Anonimalle MS, fos 269–270v. See Ranald Nicholson, *Edward III and the Scots* (Oxford, 1965), pp. 108, 116, 140.

to the abbey at that time.[67] As far as 1328 the text in the Lyell manuscript is fuller than any text other than that in the Brotherton manuscript. It may be more than a coincidence that the two fullest accounts of the reign of Edward II found in the short continuations of the prose *Brut* chronicle are in manuscripts which at one stage were in the possession of St Mary's, York. Yet the Lyell text of the short continuation is independent of the Brotherton text, and, since it was only later acquired by the abbey, it seems probable that like the Brotherton text itself it originated outside St Mary's.

As regards the relationship between the short continuation and other Edward II narratives it is clear that the short continuation was composed independently of the second and longer *Brut* continuation. Though both narratives deal broadly with the same episodes, and both are Lancastrian in sympathy, their wording and style establish the two as independent compositions. It is possible that the short continuation is the earlier of the two, and was written before the *Brut* continuations had developed their own tradition. Unlike the long continuation, the Edward II section of the short continuation appears to have been composed close to the events which it describes. The long continuation, for example, describes the murder of Edward II in some detail, while the text of the short continuation glosses the event, and in certain copies states that Edward's death was due to grief. The Anonimalle text says simply that he became ill and died. It may be that the short continuation, with its more circumspect narrative, was the earlier of the two accounts. From its character and contents it is conceivable that the short continuation was originally compiled independently of the *Brut* tradition, and only at a later stage was attached to the main text of the prose *Brut*. As a *Brut* continuation its life was limited. It was quickly superseded by the second continuation which conformed more closely to the *Brut*'s format. Nonetheless the influence of this early continuation over the second and better known narrative can possibly be inferred, especially as York appears to have been for a time the home of both authors. The northern interest seen in the concluding portion of the short continuation has been mentioned. The longer narrative is more northern in outlook

---

[67] *Anonimalle Chronicle*, p. xv, n.3. The manuscript is described under the title of Martinus Polonus by N. Ker, *Medieval Libraries of Great Britain* (London, 1964), p. 217. See Brereton, *Des Grantz Geanz*, p. xi. This copy of the short continuation contains the verse prologue.

still. It reveals little of the familiarity with London affairs which is a feature of the short continuation, and in its Edward II narrative it relates a number of northern episodes. The account of the execution of Thomas of Lancaster may, for example, rely upon the evidence of eye witnesses.[68] Such northern events as the Scottish campaign of 1322, and the execution of Andrew Harclay are described in detail.[69] It is conceivable that the entire text of the long continuation was composed at York during the 1330s, possibly by a clerk attached to a writing office close to the central administration. It is unlikely that such an author, writing a formal continuation of the prose *Brut*, would have been unaware of the earlier text, particularly if that text also had been completed at York. It may be more than a coincidence therefore that both continuations conclude at much the same point during the early years of Edward III.

The short continuation was used by a number of fourteenth-century chroniclers. It may suffice here simply to indicate the main chronicles which appear in some manner to be related to or indebted to its text.[70] Thus a number of passages in the *Brut* continuation are similar to entries in the *Gesta Edwardi de Carnarvan*, which was written in its first version *c.* 1330 by an unknown canon of Bridlington. It is difficult to be certain how these two texts are related.[71] At the end of the century Henry Knighton, the Austin canon of St Mary's, Leicester, and Thomas Burton, the one-time Cistercian abbot of Meaux, used the text of the short continuation as one source for their retrospective histories. Undoubtedly the greatest use of the continuation is seen, however, in the *Croniques de London*, one of the few London chronicles to survive from the first half of the fourteenth century. The *Croniques* appear to have been completed some ten years after the *Brut* continuation was written. Where there are similar passages the *Brut* continuation must be the source of the London account.[72] A comparison of the two reveals that there are a number of entries where the compiler of the *Croniques* drew on the short continuation for his description of national events. These passages occur mainly between 1312 and 1327. An early comparison made on the

---

[68] See *Historical Writing*, II, 73–5.
[69] *Brut*, I, 224–8.
[70] For a fuller discussion of the use of the short continuation as a source see Appendix 1.
[71] See Appendix 1.
[72] See D. C. Cox, 'The French Chronicle of London' (*Medium Aevum*, 45, 1976), pp. 203, 205.

basis of the text of the continuation in BL MS Cleopatra
D. VII, which is by no means the fullest version of the *Brut*
text, did not reveal the full relationship between the two. It is
clear from a study of the fuller versions of the short continuation,
notably the Brotherton copy, that the London chronicler was
more indebted to the *Brut* continuation than was previously
supposed.[73]

---

[73] Ibid. p. 206. See Appendix 1.

3. The Reign of Edward II and the early years of Edward III

The reign of Edward II is generally seen, and with some justice, as one of twenty years of disaster. Constant conflict between the king and members of his baronage led to periods of civil war and to the first deposition of an English king. The wars against Scotland and France were complete failures. The period, as reflected in political poetry, was one of increasing protest at economic hardship, oppressive taxes, and corruption in all levels of government. Although there were no major clashes between the king and the church, there were individual clashes between the king and bishops. The church moreover was in an unhappy state with the trial and abolition of the Order of Knights Templar, and accusations of heresy against the pope himself. The north of England, including Yorkshire, was particularly badly hit by the failures against the Scots, which prompted damaging raids as far as Bridlington, Ripon, and the Wharfe valley; York, however, benefited at times by becoming a second administrative capital when the whole government moved northwards to cope with the war. Several major political incidents were also played out in Yorkshire. Gaveston was captured at Scarborough in 1312. Then, during the period of unrest against the Despensers in 1321–2, Lancaster held important political meetings in Doncaster and Sherburn-in-Elmet. The rebels fled to join him at Pontefract; they were defeated at Boroughbridge; and Lancaster was sentenced to death for treason in his own castle at Pontefract. With hindsight, it is possible to see the bright spots of the reign. Parliament became stronger as it became a regular forum for political debate and dispute, and the commons became a regular part of it. The structure of government administration and law underwent some reform and continued to develop efficiency. Moreover this was one of the most brilliant and inventive periods of English architecture, producing the lavish extremes of the decorated style, and the dramatic experiments of the Wells Cathedral crossing arches, the Ely Cathedral octagon, and the great spire at Salisbury. But these were not what many contemporaries saw and wrote about. To them politics and warfare were the main events to record, and these were uniformly depressing.

There are still debates over a number of matters in Edward's reign: over the exact significance of his inheritance from Edward I, over his character, and over the balance of personal rivalries and constitutional ideas in the motives of the shifting groups who opposed him. For over half a century before the 1970s views of the reign were deeply influenced by the writing of Stubbs on the constitutional aspects of the opposition, then of Conway Davies and of Tout who argued for the importance of differing ideas on government and household administration in the clashes between Edward and his baronial opponents. Edward's laziness, his reliance on an inner circle of favourites and household administrators, especially his inordinate love of Piers Gaveston, and his support of the greedy and ambitious Despensers were contrasted with the high ideals of the 'Lancastrian party' and the moderating influence of the 'middle party'. Recently renewed interest in the reign has brought new interpretations. Detailed studies of the reign of Edward I allow clearer assessment of the situation at Edward II's accession; politics have been approached through studies of individuals; of the earls of Lancaster and Pembroke, of the bishops of Hereford, Exeter, Winchester, and of the archbishop of Canterbury. These have emphasised the personal element in many clashes, and forced a re-examination of the constitutional aspects. They particularly question the validity of concepts of a consistent 'Lancastrian party' and 'middle party'. Now, while it can still be acknowledged that the king, his advisers, the baronage, gentry, bishops, and no doubt the lower classes too held strong though varied views about what made 'good government', it can also be seen clearly that all were also swayed by personal interests, fears, affiliations, or hostilities. At last a more realistic and balanced view is possible of the events of Edward's reign, and of the problems that he both met and created.[74]

---

[74] For older views see W. Stubbs, *Constitutional History of Medieval England*, 3 vols. (9th ed. Oxford, 1929); T. F. Tout, *The Place of the Reign of Edward II in English History* (Manchester, 1914); J. Conway Davies, *The Baronial Opposition to Edward II* (Cambridge, 1918). For more recent ones see J. R. Maddicott, *Thomas of Lancaster, 1307–1322* (Oxford, 1970); J. R. S. Phillips, *Aymer de Valence, Earl of Pembroke, 1307–1324* (Oxford, 1972); N. Fryde, *The Tyranny and Fall of Edward II* (Cambridge, 1979); M. Buck, *Politics, Finance and the Church in the Reign of Edward II* (Cambridge, 1983). Edward's inheritance is examined in M. Prestwich, *Edward I* (1988).

Edward II's inheritance was more difficult than was once thought. He was bequeathed a government with a sophisticated structure, new regular financial resources in the customs duties and parliamentary subsidies which transformed the king's financial position, and a tradition of strong kingship and military success in Wales and France. However he was also bequeathed a huge debt of £200,000, a Scottish war which was looking ever more difficult to win, and a baronage wary of oppressive royal demands and with a recent history of open opposition to the king's wishes. Edward coped with the first problem quite well, but with the other two very badly.

Despite underlying economic difficulties, price inflation from an influx of silver, a trade slump in the middle years of the reign, and the most devastating famine of the middle ages between 1315 and 1318, Edward by the end of his reign had paid all but £60,000 of his father's debt, and had about the same sum in hand in cash. By the end of the reign, too, the effects of the famine and a subsequent sheep and cattle murrain were over, and international trade was beginning to expand once more. Edward was, as chroniclers remarked, richer than any king since the Conqueror,[75] but this success was not unalloyed. His riches were greatly criticised as the outcome of the greed of himself and his advisers, notably the two Despensers, but also his treasurer, Walter Stapledon, and his chancellor, Robert Baldock. All met violent ends in the coup of 1326–7.

The problem of Scotland was essentially a recent one. Edward I's political decisions in the years after the death of the Scottish heiress in 1290 had changed Scotland from a friendly neighbour to an open enemy, which he was trying to conquer. There is debate as to whether even Edward I himself could have achieved the permanent subjection of Scotland, but it is certain that Edward II proved completely incapable of doing so, and failure in Scotland dogged him throughout his reign. In the first years, through lack of campaigns, he allowed Robert Bruce to strengthen his hold, and in attempting to relieve Stirling in 1314 he met resounding defeat at Bannockburn. This proved a major turning point, with the Scots going on to the offensive. Scottish armies year after year raided deep into England, at times as far as Yorkshire, and took great tributes, almost amounting to regular taxation, from the northern

---

[75] *Vita*, p. 136; *Brut*, I, 225.

counties desperate to save their land from devastation. Berwick, taken by Edward I in 1296, fell again to the Scots in 1318, along with a number of border castles, and attempts to recapture Berwick in 1319 and 1322 were utter fiascoes. In 1319 not only did dissension between Lancaster and Edward impede the campaign, but to divert attention from Berwick a Scottish raid came south nearly to York. The archbishop of York, the abbot of Selby, and the mayor of York met it with a pitifully untrained force at Myton-on-Swale and were comprehensively routed. Then in 1322, when Edward's forces, badly supplied and near starvation, were forced to withdraw, the Scots chased Edward into Yorkshire and nearly captured him near Byland, prompting caustic comments from the Bridlington chronicler on a king forced to flee in his own country, and from the Lanercost chronicler who referred to him as 'ever chicken-hearted and luckless in war'.[76] The situation was so dreadful in the north that Andrew Harclay, a lifelong career soldier on the border, a royalist, and recently created earl of Carlisle for his defeat of Lancaster at Boroughbridge, took it on himself without adequate royal permission to negotiate terms for a truce with the Scots in 1323. For this treason Edward had him executed, but Edward himself made a truce the following year, and the final treaty made by Queen Isabella for Edward III in 1328 reflected closely the terms Harclay had envisaged. The problem of Scotland, however, was not then over. The treaty was unpopular with many English lords, who had had grants of land in Scotland from Edward I, and with the young and militant Edward III, and before long excuse was found to reopen the war and to replace Bruce's son with Edward Balliol, as an English client king. The great success of the English at the battle of Halidon Hill and the surrender of Berwick in 1333, fully recorded in the Anonimalle Chronicle below, went some way to expunging the memory of Bannockburn in the previous reign.

Part of Edward II's problem in fighting the Scots was his inability to bring to the war both his own undivided attention and fully united baronial support. Edward's inability throughout his reign to find a basis for permanent and trusting cooperation with his baronage proved his greatest problem.

---

[76] *Brid*, p. 81; *Lanercost*, pp. 247–8; as translated by Sir Herbert Maxwell, *The Chronicle of Lanercost, 1272–1346* (Glasgow, 1913), reprinted in *EHD*, III, 278.

He had inherited from his father a baronage which had shown willingness, between 1297 and 1307, to oppose arbitrary demands even from a respected king, and the insistence on a new clause in the coronation oath, which was meant to restrain the king from acting against the advice of his barons, undoubtedly reflected their memories of events in 1297–1307. On the other hand, the leaders of the opposition in 1297, Hereford and Norfolk, were dead, and there is no evidence that any barons were openly obstructive to the Crown in 1307. They began the reign in cooperation with the new king, accepting the return of Gaveston from exile and his creation as earl of Cornwall, although some may have had reservations. The natural assumption of the magnates was that the king would rule and they would obey, but that they would have an important public political role; as the author of the *Vita Edwardi Secundi* wrote, 'they are a chief constituent of monarchy, and without them the king cannot attempt or accomplish anything of importance'.[77] The baronage expected Edward to act with the advice and consent of the political community of the realm (by which they meant a considerable number of themselves, the bishops, and perhaps of lesser lords too). They certainly did not mean just with the help of a small group of courtiers, or worse still of one favourite, who might also control access to the king and to the springs of patronage which was so important in medieval politics. Unfortunately Edward consistently failed to do this; throughout his reign he preferred to rely on favourites, and so turned a prickly inheritance into a major problem. The position was exacerbated by the uncompromising hostility after the early years of his cousin, Thomas of Lancaster. Despite their natural willingness to work with their anointed king, other earls and barons often found themselves pulled into opposition. Opposition groups were not consistent, coalescing and breaking up according to individual interpretations of ideas of good government and to current personal rivalries and friendships, but Edward rarely enjoyed the wholehearted support of his greatest subjects after the first few months of his reign. His reliance on favourites, together with reports on his late rising, his love of music, plays, and what some chroniclers dismissed as agricultural pursuits have led to views of him as lazy, incompetent, and

[77] *Vita*, p. 28.

uninterested in government. However, in his reaction to the
Ordinances, in his defence of his favourites, and in his
acquisition of wealth, Edward showed himself not uninterested
but sharply aware of all the rights of kingship. Unfortunately
he seemed to the baronage to want the rights without fulfilling
the duties.

Edward's love for his first favourite, Piers Gaveston, led to
the first great crisis in 1310–11. The relationship was no doubt
homosexual, but the real objections to Gaveston were the
lavishness of the gifts from the king which clearly distorted the
normal pattern of court patronage, and Gaveston's own
arrogant flaunting of his position. Indeed the well-informed
author of the *Vita Edwardi Secundi* was of the opinion that if
only Piers had been a little more discreet in his attitude to the
old aristocracy, his relationship with Edward need not have
caused a crisis.[78] Objections to Gaveston culminated in the king
being forced to agree to set up a reform committee and accept
its Ordinances, presented in 1311.[79] These illustrate the mixture
of personal and constitutional grievances that the opposition
to Edward always incorporated. Some clauses sought to
remedy uncontroversial administrative defects dating well back
into Edward I's reign, others expelled from the court unpopular
indviduals including Gaveston, and yet others, clearly intended
to prevent the recurrence of arbitrary actions which had been
taken by Edward I as much as Edward II, closely touched the
king's prerogative in demanding baronial consent in parliament
for royal appointments, and for the declaration of war. Many
of the subsequent political events between 1311 and 1322 can
be seen as a struggle over the Ordinances, with Edward at one
extreme wanting to ignore or annul them, and the earl of
Lancaster at the other extreme demanding their complete
implementation. Edward and Lancaster were also divided by
bitter personal antipathy after Lancaster and Warwick had had
Gaveston executed (or murdered, depending on the point of
view) in 1312. The king never forgave Lancaster, and Lancaster
never felt safe at court. On several occasions between 1312 and
1321 open civil war between them seemed a possibility but was
averted by the mediation of more moderate earls, such as
Pembroke, or by the bishops. In the disastrous years after the

[78] *Vita*, pp. 14–15.
[79] *EHD*, III, 527–39.

defeat at Bannockburn Edward was forced to make an accommodation with Lancaster and to try to bring unity to the country. Lancaster was made head of the council in 1316 and was given a representative on the council in 1318, but he showed no more skill in government than did Edward, and remained outside the court. Indeed, in 1318 he expressed fear of the king's new courtier group of Audley, Amory (both in fact his brothers-in-law) and Montagu, and in 1321-2 he was drawn into the rebellious opposition to Hugh Despenser.

The crisis produced by Edward's favouritism for Hugh Despenser in 1321 was different from that of 1310. The opposition to Despenser was not then as universal as that against Gaveston. Despenser was English, of a perfectly respectable baronial family; his father served Edward I and Edward II well; and although his influence with Edward was growing, its danger in 1321 was fully visible as yet mainly in the Welsh Marches, where Despenser was trying to round out his lands, acquired through his wife, one of the three heiresses to the great Gloucester estates. The earl of Hereford and some Marcher lords managed to raise enough support to have Despenser exiled in 1321, but put themselves in the wrong by attacking Despenser's lands on the way to the parliament at which this was done. Edward, as determined as before to recall his friends, found it relatively easy to isolate the rebels, and marched against them with the support of all other earls except Lancaster. Lancaster himself had stood aloof from joining the rebels, although he was in touch with them, but they fled northwards hoping for support from the rich royal cousin, holder of five earldoms, and stalwart opponent of royal favourites, and he was drawn in. Meetings at Doncaster and at Sherburn-in-Elmet had shown Lancaster that the north would not rise with him: there were few in England at that time willing to take up arms openly against their anointed king. Hereford and Lancaster therefore retreated further north with diminishing troops and were defeated at Boroughbridge in March 1322 on their way between Lancaster's castles of Pontefract and Dunstanburgh.

After Boroughbridge Edward was firmly back in the saddle. The Ordinances were annulled, his opponents destroyed, and no one dared openly oppose the king; but the strength was illusory. Fear and hatred of the government and the Despensers grew, and the events of the following years led directly to deposition. The summary trial of Lancaster and his followers might have been justified under martial law,[80] but never before had so many been executed after a rebellion, nor had such a deliberate attempt been made to make this visible, by sending chosen men to their own areas for execution. The extreme revenge was remarked on in all chronicles of the time, and Lancaster's own faults were forgotten in the increasing image of him as the just man upholding the Ordinances against an arbitrary king. He was popularly seen as a martyr and miracles were reported both at his grave in Pontefract, and at the carved memorial board he had had put up to commemorate the Ordinances in St Paul's Cathedral. In the following years the failure to take Berwick in 1322, the ignominious truce with the Scots, the failure to defend Gascony against the French in 1324, quarrels with individual bishops, the increasing awareness of the riches and wilfulness of the king, and above all the greed and violence of Hugh Despenser led to great dissatisfaction with Edward and his government. The younger Despenser knew he was hated and was wary of being left alone in England if the king went abroad. It was said in the chronicles then that no one dared move into open opposition in England for fear of the consequences,[81] but it was also because few great figures were left who might lead any opposition. The earls of Lancaster and Hereford were dead and their lands forfeit; Warwick had died in 1315 leaving an heir one year old; Pembroke, a greater statesman and moderating influence, died in 1324 with no heir; Richmond, now in his 50s, was a soldier rather than a politician; Oxford, now in his late 60s, had never been active in politics; Kent and Norfolk were the king's half-brothers; Arundel, whose son was married to Despenser's daughter, was a close friend of the king and of the Despensers, and indeed was executed for his association with their regime.

The end came in 1326 with a coup led from within the royal family itself. Queen Isabella had been sent to France to negotiate peace over Gascony with her brother, the king of France, and was joined by the future Edward III who was to do homage and receive Gascony as part of the peace settlement. There they met the substantial number of disaffected lords, including Roger Mortimer, who had fled overseas after 1322. Isabella at

---

[80] M. Keen, 'Treason Trials under the Law of Arms' (*Transactions of the Royal Historical Society*, 5th series, 12, 1962), pp. 85–103.

[81] *Vita*, p. 136.

first refused to return to England unless Despenser was removed from court, but then decided to return with an armed force, ostensibly to oust the Despensers and regain her own lands. She found plenty of sympathy for these aims in the eastern counties when she landed, and also at London once Edward and the Despensers had fled westwards and the Londoners felt free to express their feelings. Rioters murdered the unpopular treasurer, Walter Stapledon, bishop of Exeter. The queen pursued the king westwards, but the king refused to leave Despenser and the queen's forces took violent action against them, capturing the king, and executing both Despensers and the earl of Arundel as summarily as these had executed their opponents in 1322. This violence put the queen and her advisers in a dilemma: the king had never before given in to violent opposition and was unlikely to do so this time. Now, if not before, his deposition must have appeared the only safe solution for his opponents. This was cleverly stage-managed to involve all political groups in England, so spreading the responsibility for what was without doubt a thoroughly illegal act. Not everyone acquiesced happily: the bishops of Rochester and London clearly had reservations about deposing an anointed king, and unease is shown in the following years in reports of plots to free Edward, miracles at his tomb, and rumours that he was still alive in 1330, but the queen and her supporters found enough general support to carry the coup to its end. They were undoubtedly helped by the fact that there was a legitimate heir nearly of age.

To some extent the years 1327 to 1330 retained the political characteristics of Edward II's reign, with failure against Scotland and court politics continuing to engage chroniclers' attention. The baronage and bishops became increasingly critical of a government which let the Scots escape at Stanhope Park, which then made a treaty with the Scots, giving up all Edward I had been fighting for, and in which a favourite, now Roger Mortimer the queen's lover, again had too much influence on patronage and the person of the king. Lancaster's brother and heir, Henry, a far more moderate and able politician than Thomas, had been appointed head of the regency council, but found himself unable to gain access to the king in the face of Mortimer's power. His stand in 1328 was on the familiar mixture of personal action against Mortimer, and principled action in favour of just and unextravagant government with baronial counsel. He failed in his action, but Mortimer, favourite of the king's mother rather than the king himself, clearly had not then the power to destroy Henry, who throughout maintained that he acted on behalf of the king. Mortimer was more successful against Kent, who was duped into thinking Edward II was still alive and so into treason. Since Kent had been an early supporter of Isabella and Mortimer in 1326, his willingness to think of reinstating Edward II indicates how Isabella and Mortimer in their turn proved unable to keep their support. Mortimer's ascendancy could only be short since Edward would soon come of age, and perhaps it was this appreciation which prompted the rumours that Mortimer intended to take the throne. Whether he had such plans or not, Mortimer was removed dramatically and suddenly in October 1330 by a coup led by Edward III himself, who then took over his government about a month short of his eighteenth birthday. He did not, at least until old age, repeat the mistakes of his father. He worked well with his baronage, and proved a successful military figure in Scotland and France. The final pages of the section of the Anonimalle Chronicle printed below reflect the change: from 1330–1334 what mattered to England was no longer internal court politics but the successes in Scotland and the final recovery of Berwick which Edward II had lost in 1318.

4. Historical value of the Anonimalle narrative

As shown in section 2 the Anonimalle narrative printed below consists of the fullest known short continuation of the French prose *Brut*, with some interpolations mainly of Franciscan, episcopal, and northern interest, from 1307 to the early part of 1333. To this has been added, probably at St Mary's itself, a detailed account of the Scottish campaign of 1333, together with some notices of episcopal appointments to bridge the gap between the end of the short continuation and the beginning of the version of the Lanercost chronicle which the compiler then used.

The usefulness of the short continuation of the French prose *Brut* has been acknowledged by modern historians for some time, and recent works on the reign of Edward II by Buck, Cam, Fryde, and Maddicott have all cited versions of it.[82] As a popular contemporary account of the years 1307–33, which would both reflect and mould popular views of the period, its content and attitudes are interesting. Although possibly written by a government clerk, it shows muted sympathy for Lancaster, a steady hatred of the Despensers, criticism of Edward II, sympathy to Isabella at least in 1326–7, and a great interest in the new English success in Scotland from 1330. Its author showed a sound understanding of the main political events of the period, and the chronicle offers some unique details both for London affairs and for the North. The account of the Scottish campaign which follows the short continuation of the *Brut* in the Anonimalle manuscript is also particularly interesting for its detail of negotiations over Berwick and its description of the Scottish army at Halidon Hill.[83]

The short continuation, in contrast to the long continuation of the *Brut*, is a sober and factual chronicle and on the whole it is an accurate account. Where it can be checked it is generally very good on names, places and documents cited. Its chronology of events is good, apart from three short sections in 1318, 1332–3, and 1333–4. In the Anonimalle text it is much more extensively dated than in other texts, which lack both the year

[82] Buck, *Politics, Finance and the Church*; H. Cam, *The London Eyre of 1321* (Selden Society, 85, 1968); Fryde, *Tyranny and Fall*; Maddicott, *Lancaster*; they have variously used Bodleian Library MSS Douce 128 and Lyell 17, and CUL MS Gg.1.15, but not the Anonimalle manuscript.
[83] See pp. 57–60 for its composition for 1333–4.

dates found here and some of the internal dates. The dating too is usually accurate, but there are a few errors which present initial problems. First the events concerning the Ordinances are telescoped and no annual dates are given between 1308 and 1312. The annual dates are then correct from 1312 to 1321, but thereafter from 1321 to 1326 all the years are begun too early: this seems to have been the result of confusion over turning the year 1321–2 when the compiler, perhaps of the Anonimalle manuscript itself, tried to provide the dates for the deaths of Bishop Langton in 1321 and the French king in January 1322 without upsetting the flow of the narrative of the civil war. From 1326 to 1333 the annual dating is again correct. Finally dates for 1333 and 1334 have been transposed although the chronology of events over the two years is correct. This transposition, together with some errors in 1334–5 at the beginning of the section already published by Professor Galbraith, seems to be caused by independent composition after the end of the short continuation; the compiler has merged sources clumsily. Once noticed, however, these errors in annual dating are no problem in the use of the text.

The chronicle usually follows the common medieval practice of starting the year at the Annunciation, 25 March, but in 1329 it has already, perhaps in error, started the new year by 13 January. Dates within the year are frequently given, normally using the system of dating by saints' days, but occasionally by days of the month. Roman dates seem to be a particular feature of the Anonimalle manuscript, and are not found in the other major versions of the short continuation. The great majority of the internal dates are accurate where they can be checked. Occasionally they are a day or two out, but often this could be because of a copyist omitting phrases such as 'the Monday after', or 'the day before'. A few uncheckable local dates are likely to be correct, as for instance the date of Chigwell's arrival in London in 1323 given as 15 September. Since his pardon was dated 5 September at Barnard Castle, where he had still been following the court, he might well have taken ten days to ride to London.[84] Some dates have recently been questioned, for instance that of the assault on Berwick in 1319, but the

---

[84] CPR 1321–4, p. 342; G. A. Williams, *Medieval London; From Commune to Capital* (London, 1963), pp. 293–4. See p. 116.

chronicle is in good company alongside the normally well-informed Lanercost chronicle in giving 15 August.[85] Overall only a dozen or so large inaccuracies appear out of over a hundred dates given, and at least one of those is clearly a faulty glossing in this text of an originally accurate date. Isabella's invasion is said to be on the 'Wednesday before Michaelmas which was on a Monday'. This was 24 September and is correct, but then in the Anonimalle text an extra phrase 'which was 4 October' has been added which is clear nonsense, and reached by counting five days on instead of five days back from Michaelmas. Although each date needs to be checked, where no other date is known then the historian may, with due caution, use the dates of this chronicle.

The short continuation begins with a preamble on the character of Edward II reminiscent of the author of the *Vita* in his later pages, emphasising Edward's self-indulgence, fickleness, vengefulness and reliance on flatterers. It provides a simple list of events for 1307–8, but then takes up a theme and under 1308 assumes under one opposition movement all the events leading to the Ordinances. Although the year-dating is not complete, this very concise passage shows a clear understanding of the background to the final publication of the Ordinances. The chronicle already shows its Lancastrian sympathy by associating Lancaster with the Ordinances at this stage, and also makes a point of mentioning his position as steward of England; this is a claim which Lancaster first made publicly in 1307 and a position which Edward granted him in 1308, but Lancaster did not use it again until 1317, and then more explicitly in 1319 in an attempt to establish a right to interfere in military organisation and in household appointments.[86] Its inclusion perhaps indicates an author interested in the more theoretical political ideas of the time. Throughout, the chronicle assumes the total validity of the Ordinances and that the prime concern was to remove Gaveston. This Anonimalle text is one of the few chronicles (along with those of Lanercost and St Paul's and the *Vita*) to specify that Gaveston spent his exile in Flanders; other texts of the short continuation

---

[85] Maddicott, *Lancaster*, p. 247; *Lanercost*, p. 239.
[86] Maddicott, *Lancaster*, pp. 76–7, 241–3; MS Lyell 17, fo. 112 links the stewardship with Thomas's holding of the earldom of Leicester at this point; the *Vita*, p. 81, is the only other chronicle to make a point of Lancaster's stewardship in 1317.

send him to Ireland, as in his exile of 1309.[87] A note on the end
of the Council of Vienne in 1312 is interpolated here in the
Anonimalle text. The short continuation then carries the story
of Gaveston's downfall through to his execution in 1312. It
makes no reference to his northern movements or his
capture at Scarborough, and incorrectly places his capture at
Deddington a week later than most other chronicles, but it
offers the exceptional detail that he was taken to Elmley, the
earl of Warwick's major Worcestershire estate, before being
moved to Warwick Castle.

Other entries for 1312 and 1313 are few. It is perhaps
interesting that there is no comment on Reynolds's appointment
to the archbishopric of Canterbury, an event which most
religious chroniclers note in order to deplore. Of some interest
is the comment on Edward's visit to France for the coronation
of the king of Navarre. The author of the *Vita* criticised Edward
for going while there were dangers from Scotland and for
using the visit to delay negotiations with the barons, and the
Annales Paulini noted a great entourage of 200 knights taken
by Edward,[88] but few other chronicles record the journey. This
is the only one to comment precisely on the extravagance of
the visit, alleging £60,000 spent in less than two months.

The account of Bannockburn is correctly dated and has the
usual list of casualties. Unlike many accounts it apportions no
blame and offers no comment. The account of the battle is
followed by a piece of purely London local interest – the
replacing of the spire of St Paul's. The detail provided is almost
as great as in the *Annales Paulini* themselves.[89] An interpolated
comment on the flood which damaged the wall of the
Franciscans' house in York in July is followed by more London
detail on the government's price fixing ordinance of 1315,
which is cited here in its London version. A number of
chronicles which mention the ordinance are critical of it: the
Bridlington chronicle is particularly scathing about men who
try to interfere with God, who alone ordains times of scarcity
and plenty.[90] This account however is the only one to chronicle
the chaotic market reaction in London to price fixing, and it

---

[87] *Lanercost*, p. 217; *Ann. Paul.*, p. 271.
[88] *Vita, pp.38–9, 42; Ann. Paul.*, p. 274.
[89] Ibid, pp. 276–7. In the Anonimalle manuscript this passage is marked by a particularly ornately
executed *nota* in the margin.
[90] *Brid.*, pp. 47–8.

emphasises that the foolish action was taken by the king and his 'weak' council, without the assent of the Ordainers and wise men of the realm.[91] From those events the chronicle moves naturally into the famine years noting the constant rain from Pentecost to the following Easter, and a three year famine. This is one of the passages clearly reflected in the chronicle of Meaux Abbey,[92] although that chronicle does not transcribe the whole passage, not being interested in the London detail that two small onions cost one penny in Cheapside.

The politics of 1316 and the heavy Scottish raids in the north after Bannockburn make no impression on the author. For 1317 he records the scandal of Gilbert Middleton's seizure of the two cardinals, Gauceline d'Euse and Lucas dei Fieschi, who had been sent to encourage peace between England and Scotland or, if that was impossible, to excommunicate the Scots. He particularly notes that Middleton was tried and executed in London early in 1318. He notes the abduction of Lancaster's wife in May 1317, but adds nothing whatever to our knowledge of its circumstances.

The subsequent piece on Despenser's election as chamberlain is interesting as the date of his appointment is still unknown, and the only certainty is that Charlton was in office at least to 19 April 1318.[93] Unfortunately this passage is one of those of confused chronology, and seems to transpose the parliament at York and the meeting at Northampton in 1318. The first section, although given under 1317, clearly refers to a period after the execution of Middleton in February 1318 and must indicate the York parliament of October 1318, where Despenser was confirmed as chamberlain by the committee set up to amend the king's household. The text then launches into a diatribe against Despenser, unusual only in being placed so early; most chroniclers insert such a passage under 1321 or 1325–6. The text then goes on, now under 1318, to assert that because of these offences the peers wanted to oust Despenser at the following Northampton parliament, but the king refused. The chronology is clearly wrong as there was no Northampton

[91] The *Annales Paulini* and *Croniques de London* do not refer to it. The London annals quote the ordinance and its revocation in full but are less descriptive of the problems caused; *Annales Londonienses*, in *Chronicles of the Reigns of Edward I and Edward II*, I, ed. W. Stubbs (RS 1882), 232–3, 237–8.

[92] *Melsa*, p. 332; Meaux's northern source noted a six year famine, *Brid*, p. 48.

[93] Tout, *Place of Edward II*, pp. 315–16; H. Cole, *Documents Illustrative of English History in the 13th and 14th Centuries* (London, 1844), p. 4.

parliament, and indeed no meeting at all at Northampton after that at York. No doubt the earlier non-parliamentary meeting held in July 1318 to negotiate with Lancaster is meant. It is unlikely that there was any general movement against Despenser then, so short a time before his confirmation at York, but it is clear that Lancaster at that time, during the negotiations which led to the treaty of Leake, was trying to purge the court of the king's favourites, including Amory, Audley, Montagu, and Despenser. Possibly some lords advised the king to remove Despenser at that point to facilitate a reconciliation with Lancaster. If so, the passage is important in its implication that Despenser was already chamberlain by July 1318. Some of the abbreviated fifteenth-century versions of the short continuation assert clearly that magnates did try to oust Despenser at Northampton, and that he had been appointed by then.[94]

The next section contains one of the fullest narratives of the impostor who claimed the throne in the great political unrest of 1317–18. The story also appears in the long continuation, the *Vita*, the chronicles of St Paul's, Bridlington, Lanercost (which adds much comment), and a number of others;[95] it did not reach the author of the *Flores*, Trokelowe, Murimuth, Le Baker, or the *Croniques de London*. The short continuation is one of three chronicles to name the impostor, (the long continuation calls him John Tanner, and the Lanercost chronicle John of Powderham); it is the only one to record him as the son of an Exeter tanner, and to have his parents summoned to testify to his birth. Three others also note him as an Oxford scribe, and all agree he first appeared at the king's hall or palace at Oxford which had recently been granted to the Carmelites. The Anonimalle text is incorrect in giving it to the 'freres cordeilles': other texts rightly record 'freres carmes'.[96] All agree that he was sent to Northampton (except the Bridlington chronicle which sent him to Nottingham), but only the short continuation records the king's wish to treat him as a fool. All

---

[94] For narrative see Maddicott, *Lancaster*, pp. 219–30; for the later chronicles see BL Harleian MS 200, fo. 74v; Cambridge, Trinity Coll. MS R.5.32, fo. 55v; Bodleian Library, Douce MS 128, fo. 157.

[95] *Brut*, I, 208–9; *Vita*, pp. 86–7; *Ann. Paul.*, pp. 282–3; *Lanercost*, pp. 236–7; *Brid*, p. 55; *Polychronicon*, pp. 308–9; *Melsa*, pp. 335–6; *Chroniques de Sempringham*, in *Le Livere de Reis de Brittanie*, ed. J. Glover (RS 1865), p. 334; *Annales de Oseneia*, in *Annales Monastici*, ed. H. R. Luard, IV (RS 1869), pp 344–5. The incident was omitted by some of the abbreviated versions of the short continuation, eg CUL MS Gg.1.15.

[96] 'Freres cordeilles' in this manuscript is an error for 'freres carmes', correctly given in other manuscripts. It may indicate the copyist's Franciscan turn of mind.

agree that he confessed to some association with the devil, but the short continuation, perhaps because of some scribal error, is the only version to give him a 'charette' as well as a cat.

The description of the siege of Berwick in 1319 is also one of the fullest in English chronicles, although most of the details in it are found separately in other accounts. The text is in good company with the Lanercost chronicle in dating the great assault to 15 August, although this date has been questioned, and with the *Vita* in explaining the reason for the siege. Clearly the siege engines made an impact on the popular mind, yet only in this chronicle are they recorded as coming from Northampton and Bamburgh, perhaps indicating that the author was a clerk then involved with ordering military supplies. Unlike some chronicles this does not expand on the internal discord of the English forces, but it does indicate it by clearly stating that the English would have taken Berwick easily if only all the lords had pulled together.[97] The description of the battle of Myton-on-Swale, during the Scottish raid to draw attention from Berwick, is fairly full, but is shorter on the actual battle tactics of the Scots than the accounts found in the long continuation and certain northern chronicles. Certain manuscripts of the short continuation are exceptional, however, in noting the name (Nicholas Fleming) of the mayor of York who was killed in the battle.[98] This version of the short continuation gives the fullest account.

The chronicle is scanty for 1320 but becomes more informative from 1321 and again shows a strong London interest, including some half dozen references to the London forces sent to the aid of the king in the 1320s.[99] Its account of the August parliament in London, at which the Despensers were exiled, is straightforward but not as full as the St Paul's annals on the baronial party, nor as the *Vita* on the negotiations.[100] It joins several chronicles in mentioning the younger Despenser's seizure of dromonds (the largest sailing ships of the time) while he was at sea, an offence listed in the accusations against him in 1326, and for which Edward III later

---

[97] See note 85; *Vita*, pp. 94–102.
[98] *Brut*, I, 211–12; *Brid.*, pp. 57–8; *Melsa*, p. 336; see above note 61. A fifteenth-century copy of the short continuation, (Bodleian Library Douce MS 128) adopts the title of 'white battle' from the long continuation.
[99] See below pp. 102, 104, 106, 110, 118–20, 122, 136. The dating slips between 1321 and 1326; see above p. 36.
[100] *Ann. Paul.*, pp. 293–7; *Vita*, pp. 112–14.

paid the Genoese compensation.[101]. It seems to be unique in having the elder Despenser curse his son, and for clearly commenting that the barons' charters of pardon from the king were useless in the face of his vengeance. It gives no clue as to the reason for the subsequent siege of Leeds Castle, the first step in Edward's counter attack against the rebels, but it does provide the fullest mention of the ensuing negotiations, when Hereford's forces came as far as Kingston-upon-Thames intending to relieve the castle. Like the *Vita*, it notes that Lancaster forbade the Marcher lords to help Badlesmere, whom Lancaster detested; like Murimuth and Le Baker it names Canterbury as the mediator (although Murimuth adds the earl of Pembroke, and Le Baker the bishop of London).[102] Uniquely it refers to Lancaster's letters to the king asking him to stop the persecution of his subjects. It is, however, mistaken in having Thomas instead of Walter Culpepper executed at Winchelsea.

The chronicle's most important point in the aftermath of the fall of Leeds Castle is its confirmation that the Marchers went immediately to Pontefract to ask Lancaster for help. This journey fits neatly with a meeting at Doncaster on or near 29 November, and with Lancaster's letter to London from Pontefract on 2 December. However the reference to the Marchers besieging Tickhill at this time, then returning to Lancaster, before moving south against the Despenser lands once more seems to be an anticipation of the siege which took place after the battle at Burton-on-Trent. In fact Hereford seems already to have been at Gloucester by 8 December, and the siege of Tickhill did not begin until about 10 January 1322.[103] The account of the Mortimers' surrender is interesting from the point of view of the relationship between this chronicle and that of Meaux. The short continuation text may seem to suggest that friars (*freres*) were involved in the negotiations with the Mortimers; the abbot of Meaux certainly read the passage thus, and even elaborated on it, making them *fratres mendicantes*. This is, however, quite wrong: other chronicles

---

[101] The accusation about plundering the dromonds was repeated in the accusations against Despenser in 1326 (John Taylor, 'The judgement on Hugh Despenser the Younger' (*Medievalia et Humanistica*, 1958, pp. 70–7); the Genoese claimed damages of 14,300 marks, and in 1336 Edward III, of his grace but denying his liability, granted them compensation of 8,000 marks; *CCR 1333–7*, pp. 686–7.

[102] *Vita*, p. 116; *Murimuth*, p. 34; *Le Baker*, p. 12; see also *Ann. Paul.*, pp. 299–300.

[103] Maddicott, *Lancaster*, pp. 297–307.

make clear that the go-betweens were magnates, and the safe-conduct for the Mortimers shows that it was requested by magnates, including Norfolk and Kent, the king's brothers. The *freres* of the short continuation were clearly these brothers, and a copyist's omission of their names, or their relationship with the king, led the abbot of Meaux into error. The date given here for the surrender, 25 January, may be two days too late, as the known safe-conduct for the Mortimers ran out on 23 January.[104]

The continued London interest is apparent in the mention of 380 Londoners sent to Worcester and a further 120 sent to the king in March for his campaign against Hereford and Lancaster. The chronicle is exceptional in its note that at this time the Londoners preferred the baronial cause but feared the king, and is certainly correct. The city disliked the judicial eyre set up in London in 1321, for which it blamed Despenser, and the London letter book for the period indicates the cautious bargaining over men-at-arms to be sent to the King carried on by Chigwell, then mayor of London, which confirms a less than whole-hearted support from the city.[105]

On the battle at Boroughbridge the short continuation is very concise and adds nothing new. It notes the deaths of Sully, Bromsfeld, and Elpingdon alongside Hereford, but makes no reference to the particularly unpleasant death of Hereford, which comes in the more sensational long continuation and Le Baker, and is reminiscent of their later descriptions of Edward's own death. That tale is also picked up later by the abbot of Meaux.[106] The chronicle shows more interest in the trial of Lancaster than the battle, although again the account is short. Like many chronicles it reflects the publicised proclamation of the process against Lancaster for treason, and criticises its form. Along with the long continuation and the *Annales Paulini* it correctly records Mablethorp, recently appointed a justice of the King's Bench, as one of Lancaster's judges.[107] Its sympathy for Lancaster and Hereford is clear: Lancaster is sent to his own loved castle to be executed; and like the *Vita* and Lanercost

[104] *Melsa*, p. 340; *Ann. Paul.*, p. 301; *Murimuth*, p. 35; *Parl. Writs*, II, ii, App. p. 176. The date given for the Mortimers' surrender is also that used by the *Croniques de London*, p. 43.

[105] *Calendar of the Letter Books preserved among the Archives of the Corporation of the City of London, 1275–1498*, ed. R. R. Sharpe, 11 vols. (1899–1912), *Letter Book 'E'*, pp. 153–4; Williams, *Medieval London*, pp. 288–90; Maddicott, *Lancaster*, p. 298.

[106] *Brut*, I, 219; *Le Baker*, p. 14; *Melsa*, p. 342.

[107] *Brut*, I, 222; *Ann. Paul.*, p. 302; he was appointed in 1320 (Tout, *Place of Edward II*, p. 332).

chronicle it sees Lancaster's death as revenge for Gaveston's death a decade before. The date of execution is, however, given wrongly as 20 instead of 22 March.[108] The list of those executed is extensive and drawn from the same list which circulated to many other chroniclers in all parts of England. Seventeen names are given (probably originally eighteen as the phrase on Gloucester is defective), but several chroniclers give more.[109] The shock of the scale of the executions is shown by the repetition of these lists. The continued London interest of this chronicle is shown in the precise dating, not given elsewhere, for the executions at London, Windsor, and Canterbury.

The Scottish campaign of 1322 is shortly dealt with. The Byland fiasco is reported but with no northern details and with a date too late.[110] The chronicle is rare, however, in its interest in Richmond's captivity. It is one of two English chronicles to record his ransom. Whether its figure of £3,000 is correct is unknown but the ransom was clearly huge since it took three years to raise, and Edward II even tried unsuccessfully to engage parliamentary aid. The only other English suggestion is of the larger sum of 14,000 marks in the *Flores Historiarum*. Barbour's *Bruce* suggests £2,000.[111] The chronicle is unique in giving a date for Richmond's return. It is a pity that it gives the feast of St Louis, bishop and confessor, a saint who does not seem to exist, but if St Louis, king and confessor, is meant, then the date, 25 August, is very plausible, since Richmond was still a prisoner on 4 May 1324 but was free to be summoned to Westminster on 24 September that year.[112] Like a number of other southern chronicles and some northern ones the short continuation accepts Harclay's possible treachery at Byland, and, unlike the Lanercost chronicle, it shows no sympathy for his treasonable Scottish negotiations later. His execution simply gives another opportunity to refer to God's punishment for those who harmed Lancaster. With the

---

[108] *Vita*, p. 126; *Lanercost*, p. 244; the Meaux chronicle also records 20 March (*Melsa*, p. 342).

[109] *Parl. Writs*, II, ii, App., p. 200 (29); *Flores*, III, 207–8 (22); *Croniques de London*, p. 44 and B L Cotton Cleo. D IX fos. 84v–85, as in G. L. Haskins, 'A chronicle of the civil wars of Edward II' (*Speculum*, 14, 1939), pp. 79–80 (21); *Melsa*, p. 343 (20); *Brut*, I, 224 (19).

[110] The battle took place on 14 October; Edward arrived in Bridlington the day after (*Brid.*, p. 79).

[111] *Flores*, III, 224–5; *The Bruce*, ed. W. Skeat (EETS extra series 29, 1877), pt. iii, p. 462, lines 520–2.

[112] I. Lubimenko, *Jean de Bretagne comte de Richmond. Sa vie et son activité en Angleterre, en Écosse et en France* (Paris, 1908), pp. 67–70. The only other chronicle to mention the length of Richmond's imprisonment is also a London one, *Ann. Paul.*, p. 304.

arrival of Harclay's head in London the chronicle returns for a while to London affairs.

The miracles after Lancaster's death find their fullest descriptions in this continuation, in the long continuation, the *Flores*, and the *Croniques de London*,[113] but only in this continuation and the *Flores* is there mention of the miracles in both London and Pontefract, and of the care taken to stop popular veneration of Lancaster. Here again the interest in Lancaster is strong. The chronicle then devotes considerable space to the escape of Mortimer from the Tower. It offers the fullest list of speculations about how he escaped, although the potion is mentioned by several others, and his walking through the gate by the *Flores*. Like the long continuation and the *Flores* it mentions that he escaped only just before he was to be executed.[114] The St Paul's annals give more detail on his route to escape abroad and the Londoners who helped, but the short continuation is exceptional in its reference to the accusations against the Londoners brought by Thomas Newbiggin, acting as informer. This reference appears elsewhere only in the *Croniques de London*, which was probably drawing on this source.[115]

The French war of 1324 is very cursorily treated indeed in this text, with no references to the negotiations by the earl of Kent and the archbishop of Dublin, nor to the fighting, nor to the fall of La Réole, although some other versions contain a little more detail.[116] However, it is interesting that the chronicle suggests that the king, having mustered the fleet at Portsmouth, deliberately sent it away in the autumn of 1324. Although this is incorrect there had been many delays in sending supplies to the earl of Kent, giving rise to the rumours, reflected here, that this was deliberate royal policy. Despenser, then at Porchester with the king, wrote Kent a placatory letter on 24 September 1324 denying that some of the king's counsellors were arguing

---

[113] *Brut*, I, 228–31; *Flores*, III, 213–14; *Croniques de London*, p. 46. The chronicles of *Lanercost* (pp. 244–5) and Meaux (p. 344) have shorter references. Surprisingly neither the canon of Bridlington nor the *Annales Paulini* mentions the miracles.

[114] *Brut*, I, 231; *Flores*, III, 217; *Blaneford*, pp. 145–6; see E. L. G. Stones, 'The date of Roger Mortimer's escape from the Tower of London' (*EHR*, lxvi, 1951), pp. 97–8. Blaneford's erroneous dating to 1324 and his references to both potions and ropeladders may suggest that he was using a version of the short continuation close to that of the Anonimalle Chronicle.

[115] *Ann. Paul.*, pp. 305–6; *Croniques de London*, p. 47; Williams, *Medieval London*, pp. 293–4.

[116] Three fourteenth-century versions (Bodleian Library MS Lyell 17, fo. 116; CUL MSS Gg.1.15, fo. 189, Mm.1.33, fo. 61v) note Kent's departure for Gascony, and three fifteenth-century versions which precede Avesbury's chronicle add the fall of La Réole (Bodleian Library MS Douce 128, fo. 161; Trin. Coll. Camb. MS R.5.32, fo. 56v; BL Harleian MS 200, fo. 76).

against sending supplies, and maintaining that the delays were simply because of the winds and beyond his control.[117]

There is more interest in Queen Isabella's loss of her lands and household on 18 September 1324, the blame for which was placed on Stapledon and Baldock as well as the Despensers at this stage.[118] Edward's preparations for his voyage to France in 1325 finds even more space, again with reference to the Londoners' contribution of men, and with a reference to a fleet size of 100.[119] The blame for Edward's withdrawal from the voyage is placed squarely, as in other chronicles, on Hugh Despenser's fear of being·left in England. Sympathy is shown for Isabella in the detailed description of her stay in France. This chronicle has more detail on this matter than any other single source, although no item is unique to it. Like the Lanercost chronicle and the long continuation it records the story of the attempt to bribe the French peers into sending her home, a story possibly based on letters Edward wrote to France asking that Isabella be encouraged to return.[120]

At this point the chronicler turns from matters of national interest to insert local and commercial detail important to London and its merchants. The reversal of the wool staple policy with the removal of the staple from Bruges to English towns in May 1326 was almost certainly done to keep London happy at a crucial time and the prohibition of the export of teasels and fullers' earth was clearly at the behest of Chigwell, the London mayor.[121] The short continuation, like the *Annales Paulini*, makes much of the drought in the Midlands, noting the saltiness of the Thames and the fires at Royston, Croxton, and Wandlesworth. This passage too was picked up by the Meaux chronicler, at first sight surprisingly, but Croxton, like Meaux, was a Cistercian house.[122]

---

[117] *The War of St Sardos*, ed. P. Chaplais (Camden Society, third series, 87, Royal Historical Society, 1954), p. 64.

[118] The wages allotted to the queen are recorded as 20 shillings a day in Bodleian Library MS Lyell 17, fo. 116, and *Croniques de London*, p. 48.

[119] The *Croniques de London*, p. 48, and the Meaux chronicle, p. 349, also record 100 but the *Annales Paulini*, p. 308, record 80 with a supplement of 40.

[120] *Lanercost*, p. 255; *Brut*, I, p. 234; *CCR 1323–7*, pp. 577, 578–9. The *Vita*, p. 143, also notes Isabella as a lady mourning her lord.

[121] Williams, *Medieval London*, p. 294; *Calendar of the Plea and Memoranda Rolls preserved among the Archives of the Corporation of the City of London at the Guildhall, AD 1323–1364*, ed. A. H. Thomas (Cambridge, 1926), p. 44; *Letter Book 'E'*, p. 210–11.

[122] *Ann. Paul.*, p. 313; *Melsa*, p. 349.

Isabella's invasion is dealt with shortly as in most chronicles. [123]
The precise landing place is still unknown, but this chronicle
adds weight to the argument for the north side of the Orwell.
Its description of the landing place as Harwich in Suffolk is
shared by the Bridlington chronicle and the long continuation,
but the Meaux chronicle correctly places Harwich in Essex.
Other chronicles and other texts of this continuation also record
the landing place as in Essex, and the *Annales Paulini* state that
Isabella slept that night at Walton. [124] The constant references
to Harwich and Essex, and the night at Walton (possibly
Walton-on-the-Naze) suggest the south bank of the Orwell,
but the north bank would have been more convenient for
Isabella's next stop at Bury St Edmunds. The phrase 'within
the port of Harwich' does not make this impossible as ports
had jurisdiction over coasts and river banks some distance away
from them. Moreover the king himself heard that Isabella had
landed in Suffolk. [125] Only this chronicle and the *Annales Paulini*
record the safe withdrawal of Isabella's fleet, the latter however
recording that one ship was captured by the king's men. [126]

The continuation now becomes particularly valuable for its
information on events in London. Between them this account,
the *Annales Paulini*, and the *Croniques de London*, each with
different information, provide a powerful picture of a divided,
uncertain, and violent city. [127] Many might have preferred
Isabella's cause, but the more moderate or cautious city fathers
did not immediately respond to her letters, and even after the
king had left London they were prepared to work with the
legitimate government. This version of the short continuation
together with other extended copies gives the fullest chronicle
account that we have of Isabella's letters and the city's
negotiations with the king's privy council, and it provides an
important source of information for both the *Croniques de
London* and the Meaux chronicle (the only provincial chronicle
to show any interest in London's affairs apart from the interest
aroused by the murder of Bishop Stapledon). [128] The short

[123] See p. 37 for the dating.
[124] *Brid.* p. 86; *Brut*, I, 236; *Melsa*, p. 350; *Croniques de London*, p. 51; *Murimuth*, p. 46; *Ann. Paul.*,
pp. 313–14; Bodleian Library MS Lyell 17, fo. 117 (Essex at Orwell near Harwich); CUL MS
Gg.1.15, fo. 190v (as Lyell 17); Bodleian Library MS Douce 128, fo. 162 (Essex at Orwell
haven near Ipswich).
[125] *Foedera*, II, i, 643.
[126] *Ann. Paul.*, p. 314.
[127] Ibid., pp. 315–17, 320–2; *Croniques de London*, pp. 51–5.
[128] *Melsa*, pp. 351–2.

continuation is the only chronicle to cite Isabella's second letter to the city, and it does so fully and accurately.[129] It and the chronicles which used it are the only narratives to note the attempt to by-pass the circumspect city council and to rouse the city for the queen by pinning copies of the letters to windows. It is the only description to give full information on Chigwell's meeting with the privy council at Blackfriars on the fateful 15 October, and names three members – Walter of Norwich, Hervy de Staunton, and Geoffrey le Scrope. This helps to narrow the period when Scrope finally left the king: he was clearly still supporting him on 15 October, but was given protection by Isabella in late October or early November.[130] The short continuation is also the only chronicle to underline the anger of the commonalty at Chigwell's meeting; the *Croniques de London* borrow only part of the passage and are consequently much less clear on what happened.[131] Chigwell, despite his brief period of royal disfavour, had been placed back in office after the escape of Mortimer from the Tower with Londoners' connivance, because it became clear to the government that alternatives to Chigwell were even more hostile to it. Certainly Chigwell tried to work with the king's government, but finally on 15 November, when the queen's side was clearly winning, he lost office.[132] The only apparent inaccuracy in this section is the dating of the king's departure from London as 'the day after the publication of the letter' which is placed after mention of the second letter, itself dated 6 October. By then the king was in Gloucestershire,[133] so undoubtedly Isabella's first letter is meant. Once the king had left London, the mob got out of hand. Their assassination of Stapledon was dramatic enough to be recorded in all chronicles. This account seems to offer the best description of Stapledon's last ride, although the *Croniques de London* have more on the deaths of his two followers, and

---

[129] It varies from the contemporary copy in the London plea and memoranda roll in only minor spellings and the occasional word; London Record Office, Plea and Memoranda Roll A 1b, m.10; other versions of the short continuation generally have less good and shorter copies of the letter.

[130] *Calendar of Plea and Memoranda Rolls, 1323–1364*, p. 16; E L. G. Stones, 'Sir Geoffrey le Scrope, Chief Justice of the King's Bench' (*EHR*, lxix, 1954), 1–17. *Memorials of St Edmund's Abbey*, ed T. Arnold, 3 vols. (RS 1890–6) II, 329 notes Scrope and Staunton but not Norwich as men attacked by the rioters.

[131] *Croniques de London*, pp. 51–2.

[132] Williams, *Medieval London*, pp. 295–7.

[133] *The itinerary of Edward II and his household, 1307–1328*, ed. E. M. Hallam (List and Index Society, 211, 1984), p. 290.

the *Annales Paulini* have more information on the difficulty of finding somewhere to lay the corpse.[134] The chronicle finally notes the oaths of the bishops and magnates to the city and the queen's cause, and the release of prisoners from the Tower, but it leaves further information on the rioting to the *Croniques* and the *Annales Paulini*.

The queen's pursuit of the king to Wales, the executions of the Despensers, Arundel, and Simon of Reading, and Baldock's imprisonment are all dealt with concisely and dated accurately. Like the chronicle of Lanercost, this chronicle says that Edward was trying to reach Ireland when his ship was blown to Wales.[135] It places Neath in the Snowdon area, a mistake repeated in the *Croniques de London*.[136]

The chronicle deals concisely too with the deposition, offering no real help in disentangling just what was done. It does, however, explicitly state that the archbishop of Canterbury read the articles of accusation against the king, and most texts of the short continuation, except this one, note that Edward II, when he was forced to resign his throne, gave his son his blessing. The chronicle also seems to give the best text of William Trussell's renunciation of homage to the king. The short continuation's text tallies almost exactly with the French version of the text used in the *Annales Paulini* and by Knighton, both of which omit one clause given in our manuscript; it also tallies with the Latin version of the renunciation in the normally accurate Bridlington chronicle. The short précis of the renunciation in Higden's *Polychronicon*, the *Flores*, and the Meaux chronicle belong to another tradition altogether.[137]

Clearly the most important aspect of Edward III's coronation to this chronicler was the confirmation and extension of London's franchises in the new charter of 9 March 1327. He makes a point of recording the city's new right to hang certain offenders and mentions the grant again (fo. 262v) as being 'greater than by any other king'.

---

[134] *Croniques de London*, p. 52; *Ann. Paul.*, pp. 316–17. The use of the phrase 'behind the butchery' may indicate a semi-permanent row of stalls or shops in that part of Newgate Street which was at that time a flesh market. I am indebted to Dr Vanessa Harding for this information; see E. Ekwall, *Street-names of the City of London*, (Oxford, 1954), pp. 29–30.

[135] *Lanercost*, p. 256.

[136] *Croniques de London*, p. 56; *Murimuth*, p. 49, gives Glamorgan; *Melsa*, p. 353, does not repeat the short continuation error, but gives Westwallia.

[137] Bodleian Library MS Lyell 17, fo. 118v; CUL MS Gg.1.15, fo. 194; *Ann. Paul.*, p. 324; *Knighton*, pp. 441–2; *Brid.*, p. 90; *Polychronicon*, p. 322; *Flores*, III, 325; *Melsa*, pp. 353–4.

The account of the reign of Edward II closes with a forward look to his move to Berkeley castle because of rumours of a plot to rescue him from Kenilworth by Dunheved and others, and finally with a reference to his illness and death, correctly dated to 21 September 1327. Although some other versions of this short continuation speak of his dying through grief, there is no hint in the chronicle of ill-treatment or murder. These atrocity stories belong to the next generation of chroniclers, influenced no doubt by the more colourful tales of the notoriously entertaining long continuation and of Geoffrey le Baker.[138] Nor is there anything here to suggest a successful escape; but then no contemporary chronicler doubts that Edward II died in 1327, whatever he may have to say about the manner of his dying.[139] The length of the reign given here (nineteen years, three months and two weeks) makes no sense in relation to the date of deposition or death, but twenty years, three months and two weeks would fit the day of his death. Edward's death is followed by what is almost certainly a long interpolation on papal affairs with special references to John XXII's persecution of the Franciscans. This great quarrel is recorded by most chroniclers, and placed in various years between 1325 and 1330.[140]

With the reign of Edward III the northern interest of the chronicle becomes more pronounced, and at times the detail is so exact, including the names of occupants of peels, that a northern origin seems more likely. However the London interest is still evident up to 1331 in the record of London contributions to the king's forces at Stanhope Park, the defence of London's role in Henry of Lancaster's rebellion, and in the descriptions of London tournaments.

The events at Stanhope Park are dealt with shortly and competently, adding nothing new to the details already fully explained by Dr Nicholson. The number given here of 160 London horsemen sent there is incidentally lower than that of

---

[138] See for instance Bodleian Library MS Lyell 17, fo. 118v; CUL MS Gg.1.15, fo. 194v; Trin. Coll. Camb. MS R.5.32, fo. 57v; BL Harleian MS 200, fo. 78; Brut, 1, 253; Le Baker, pp. 30–4.

[139] The possibility of Edward's successful escape is raised by the letter of Manuel de Fieschi. This is examined in T. F. Tout, 'The captivity and death of Edward of Caernarvon', Collected Papers, III (Manchester, 1934); G. P. Cuttino and T. W. Lyman, 'Where is Edward II?' (Speculum, 53, 1978),pp. 522–44; and Fryde, Tyranny and Fall, pp. 203–6.

[140] Ann. Paul., pp. 345, 350–2, places it under 1329–30; Lanercost, pp. 245–6, 251–3, 263–4, traces it through from 1322 to 1328.

200 given in the *Croniques de London*.[141] Like others, the chronicle blames the fiasco and the escape of the Scottish army on dissent between the English and Hainaulters and between the English themselves. The strong northern interest is shown in references to the subsequent attacks on Alnwick and Warkworth castles, which are mentioned elsewhere only in the chronicles of Bridlington, Meaux, and (in a more general way) of Lanercost.[142] The Scottish treaty of 1328 is similarly concisely dealt with, without the strong overt criticism found in some chronicles; but the heavy emphasis on England's return of all liberties and the Ragman Roll to Scotland implies distaste.

From the years 1328 to 1330 interest turns entirely around the major political shocks at the centre: the rebellion of Henry of Lancaster, the executions of the earl of Kent and Mortimer, and the retirement of the queen. This chronicle is one of the few to give weight to Lancaster's rising. It provides a narrative which offers context and sense, and which fits the verifiable facts. Although it lacks the full list of baronial grievances which is found in the long continuation, it does clearly bring out the two main grievances, namely that not even Lancaster, head of the regency council, could get near the king as Isabella and Mortimer had usurped royal power; and that Isabella and Mortimer had depleted the royal treasury so that the government was obliged to draw heavily on prises. The account also brings out Lancaster's support from the archbishop of Canterbury and the bishops, although it has less on the negotiations than the *Annales Paulini*. There is no specific mention of the role of Kent and Norfolk in the rising, and consequently no blame for defeat is placed on their defection, as it is later by Knighton.[143] The chronicle's continued London interest is shown by its defence of the Londoners who supported Lancaster despite their specific declaration of loyalty to the king.[144] The chronicle does not fill the gaps identified by Dr Holmes,[145] but it does confirm the impression of a certain skill

---

[141] R. Nicholson, *Edward III and the Scots* (Oxford, 1965), pp. 26–41; *Croniques de London*, p. 60; Bodleian Library MS Lyell 17, fo. 119 gives 140 horsemen.

[142] *Brid.*, p. 97; *Melsa*, p. 357; *Lanercost*, p. 260. The northern raids are omitted in some abbreviated versions of the short continuation; Bodleian Library MS Lyell 17, fo. 119 substitutes the Lincoln parliament and the announcement of Edward II's death.

[143] *Brut*, I, 257–61; *Ann. Paul.*, pp. 343–4; *Knighton*, pp. 447–8, 450–1.

[144] See also *Calendar of Plea and Memoranda Rolls, 1323–1364*, pp. 77–86.

[145] G. A. Holmes, 'The rebellion of the Earl of Lancaster, 1328–9', *BIHR* 28 (1955).

and judgment on the part of the compiler as a concise and interested political commentator.

The execution of Kent, accurately dated, is dealt with briefly and gives no indication of why he was killed. The details of the plot will never be known: the *Annales Paulini* report that *exploratores* (*agents provocateurs*) were spreading rumours that Edward II was alive abroad and would return if given help.[146] The circumstantial detail in the long continuation (which emphasised the pope's encouragement of Kent and Kent's letters to his brother), in Le Baker (who relates the bribing of the doorman and the view of Edward II feasting at Corfe), and in the Lanercost chronicle (which accepts a plot by the pope, bishops, and Dominicans) simply shows that England was rife with rumour.[147] Most chronicles accept that Mortimer engineered Kent's downfall, and this chronicle, and those indebted to it, specifically record such great pity for Kent that no executioner could at first be found.[148] Murimuth on the other hand, while explicitly accepting that Kent's confession was a fabrication, sourly said that no one regretted Kent's passing.[149]

Mortimer now had only seven months of power left and, apart from mentioning and correctly dating the birth of Edward's first son, the chronicle moves straight to Mortimer's downfall. Again the story is told straightforwardly and concisely. It has none of the elaboration of events of the long continuation, Le Baker, and the Meaux chronicle. Its only elaboration is the comment that Geoffrey Mortimer had taken his father's ambitions seriously enough to call himself king. It does not cite the articles against Mortimer at length as does Knighton,[150] but its comments on the causes of Mortimer's fall reflect the main accusations of the articles accurately, and, as with the account of Lancaster's rebellion, the author shows himself a concise and competent commentator.

1331 seems a pleasant interlude amongst the politics and wars of the period. The chronicle correctly dates Edward's journey to France to pay homage for Gascony and records some of the elaborate tournaments and jousts organised throughout the summer on his return. It includes the

---

[146] *Ann. Paul.*, p. 349.
[147] *Brut*, I, 263–7; *Le Baker*, pp. 43–4; *Lanercost*, pp. 264–5.
[148] *Knighton*, p. 452; *Melsa*, p. 359.
[149] *Murimuth*, p. 60; he is followed by *Le Baker*, p. 44.
[150] *Brut*, I, 268–72; *Le Baker*, pp. 45–8; *Melsa*, p. 360; *Knighton*, pp. 453–8; see also *Murimuth*, pp. 63–4; *Lanercost*, pp. 265–6.

fullest description of the near disaster at William Montagu's tournament in Cheapside in September, and the fullest description of the staging: clearly a wooden platform of substantial size had been set high across and above the road for the queen to view the jousts better. The account also gives local details, such as that the jousting area was between the cross at St Paul's and Soper's Lane, and that the queen was taken to recover to Nicholas Farndon's house in Wood Street. The disaster was newsworthy enough to appear in the Bridlington chronicle, but the annals of St Paul's give the accident only a short mention, preferring to spend more time on the procession and clothing for the tournament, in which the king and his knights dressed splendidly as Tartars, leading their ladies, dressed all in red velvet, on silver chains.[151]

After these London events the short continuation turns exclusively and in much detail to the Scottish wars for the next two years, possibly reflecting its authorship by a government clerk who moved with the administration to York.[152] Although official records provide most information about the organisation of the wars, historians still draw heavily on chronicles for details. The short continuation offers a full and valuable coverage and compares well with the better known northern English chronicles usually consulted for the period, some of which are considerably later in composition.

The account of the disinherited lords invading Scotland through Kinghorn in Fife, and of the battle of Dupplin Moor is good, although not as detailed on battle tactics as are the accounts in the chronicles of Bridlington and of Meaux (which here draws heavily on Bridlington), nor is the description as expansive on the English fears as is Knighton. Nevertheless it covers the essential points and is itself a source for both Knighton and the abbot of Meaux.[153] Its list of eight of the disinherited, who are named, is exceeded only by that of the canon of Bridlington who added six more and noted that their ships left from nearby Barton-on-Humber and Hull. It gives one of the highest figures (2,500) for the English forces at Dupplin Moor, a figure adopted by Knighton but not by the

---

[151] *Brid*, p. 102; *Le Baker*, p. 48; *Murimuth*, p. 63; *Ann. Paul.*, pp. 352–5. The tournament is put in context in J. R. V. Barker, *The Tournament in England, 1100–1400* (1986), pp. 98, 102.
[152] See p. 20.
[153] *Brid.*, pp. 103–7; *Melsa*, pp. 362–5; *Knighton*, pp. 461–4. Knighton's list substituted Ferrers and Wake for Angus and Ughtred; the abbot of Meaux's substituted Felton for Ughtred.

abbot of Meaux. All accounts agree that the English were greatly outnumbered both at Kinghorn and at Dupplin Moor, although estimates vary. The short continuation gives 10,000 as the figure for the Scots at Kinghorn, in common with the long continuation and Knighton, although not the Meaux chronicle. Both Knighton and the Meaux chronicle accept the figure of 900 Scottish dead. Estimates of the Scots at Dupplin Moor are much higher – most chronicles also giving the 40,000 used in this account. The description of the battle tactics is short but coherent and congruent with what has been worked out by Dr Nicholson from a variety of chronicles. This account appears to be the source of Knighton's comment on the forty German horsemen on the English side, and another text of the short continuation specifies that they stayed on horseback behind the English lines. The list of Scottish lords killed in the battle is the longest in any English chronicle and it, or a common source, was later used by Knighton and the abbot of Meaux, who also report the same numbers of Scottish dead. The list is inaccurate in including the earls of Carrick and Atholl who were both killed the following year at Halidon Hill, and in giving Alexander Bruce, earl of Carrick, as though he were two men, but this is not the only chronicle to offend in this way: possibly an exaggerated list of the dead circulated in England, and the normally accurate Lanercost chronicle was also confused over the earldom of Carrick. Knighton and the Meaux chronicle also quote exactly the list of English dead used by the short continuation.[154]

The subsequent siege of Perth and the abortive naval action of John Crabbe is again given the fullest treatment in any English chronicle, although it is almost rivalled by that of the canon of Bridlington. Knighton again used this account, while the abbot of Meaux used a combination of this narrative and information found in the Bridlington chronicle. The long continuation and the Lanercost chronicle are much shorter on these episodes, but Lanercost does explain the Scots raid on Galloway as a retaliation against raids into Scotland by Galloway men in their attempt to raise the Scottish siege of

[154] CUL MS Gg.1.15, fo. 199 for the German horsemen; see note 153 above; *Lanercost*, pp. 267–8; *Murimuth*, pp. 66–7; *Brut*,I, 274–9. The abbot of Meaux accepted Bridlington's figure of 1,500 English at Dupplin Moor. He gave the highest number for the Scots at Kinghorn with 14,000, while the Lanercost chronicle gave the lowest with 4,000. The shortest and most correct list of the Scottish earls killed at Dupplin Moor is in the canon of Bridlington's chronicle.

Perth. This chronicle, like a number of others, gives no reason for it beyond explaining that Balliol's lands were there.[155]

The success of the disinherited had been dramatic: not surprisingly Balliol thought he had enough support to be crowned on 24 September 1332, but equally unsurprisingly the support was unstable. He quickly lost Perth and was expelled from Scotland. The narrative of the events of that autumn and winter is one of the most confused passages in this text of the short continuation as the compiler seems to have combined clumsily two separate Scottish attacks, one at Roxburgh and one at Annandale. Other short continuation texts note only the Annandale raid, and it is possible that already a northern compiler, possibly at St Mary's, was introducing extra material.[156] As this is an important period which finally resulted in Edward III's open support for Balliol and led to the battle of Halidon Hill it is worth looking at this section in more detail, using the excellent secondary account pieced together by Dr Nicholson from the accounts in the Bridlington and Lanercost chronicles, the *Scalacronica*, and Scottish chronicles.[157] The chronology appears to be as follows. After the siege of Perth, Balliol went to Roxburgh and Kelso for a few days where a large group of Scots attacked him. Fighting centred on the bridge at Roxburgh, where Thomas Ughtred was particularly valiant, and Balliol's men drove off the Scots, capturing Sir Andrew Moray and John Crabbe. About this time the earls of Atholl and Buchan (Henry Beaumont) left to go to Edward III's parliament at York called for 4 December. Balliol went to Annandale for Christmas, confident in a truce made with the Scots to last until 2 February, but again he was attacked, and this time John Mowbray and Walter Comyn were killed and Balliol barely escaped to Carlisle. Edward III then gave permission for English lords to help Balliol, who re-entered Scotland and was besieging Berwick by March. The Scottish retaliation for this was a raid into Gilsland, near Carlisle, which itself brought English retaliation in a raid which took the peel of Lochmaben, and at last gave Edward an excuse to give his own support to Balliol. He marched to Berwick in May and the siege ended with the battle of Halidon Hill in July.

---

[155] *Brid.*, pp. 107–8; *Knighton* p. 464; *Melsa*, pp. 365–6; *Brut*, I, 279–80; *Lanercost*, p. 269.
[156] See for example Bodleian Library MS Lyell 17, fo. 121; CUL MS Gg.1.15, fos. 200–200v.
[157] Nicholson, *Edward III and the Scots*, pp. 96–113. The usually well-informed Lanercost chronicle does not mention the truce (pp. 270–3).

All these points and others are in this account but in confused order.[158] The chronicle takes Balliol to Roxburgh, records Ughtred's defence of the bridge, the Scottish flight and the capture of Moray, but it also mentions the truce which was asked for until 2 February, and that Balliol fled. This is clearly the ending of the Annandale incident given to the Roxburgh raid. The chronicle also wrongly has Crabbe escape to Berwick, using words very close to those which described his earlier flight from Perth to Berwick. The chronicle continues with Balliol in England after his escape and notes his return to Scotland in Lent 1333, taking the peel of Robert Colville on the way. It next relates a story, found apparently in no other chronicle, in which some English lords tried to persuade Berwick to surrender to Edward III and not to Balliol. The account now returns to the events of autumn 1332: it relates the departure of some lords for Edward's December parliament, the arrangement of the truce to 2 February (which it consciously sees as a repeat – 'autrefoiz li prierent de enduces'), and the surprise attack on Balliol. This time it gives victory to Balliol. Clearly the endings of the two raids have been transposed. The chronicle then returns to a correct chronological order, with English lords reentering Scotland with Balliol, the Gilsland and Lochmaben raids, and Edward III's entry into the war.

Such confusion may leave doubts about the chronicle's general reliability, but although misplaced in order the material itself is good, and most details are corroborated by other reliable sources. The problem lies in faulty compiling, not in faulty material. It may well be, therefore, that the chronicle should be trusted in the matters unique to it – the English attempt to negotiate separately at Berwick, and the list of English lords with Balliol at the attack on Colville's peel. The relationships of the chronicle with its borrowers and with the Lanercost chronicle are again interesting. Knighton describes the February truce in a form very similar to that in the Anonimalle manuscript, but makes no reference to Beche and Talbot. He also records the taking of Colville's peel, found in no other English chronicle except that of the continuator of 'Hemingburgh', who may also be using a short continuation as a source. The abbot of Meaux used this version of the Gilsland raid, but also took details from the Bridlington

---

[158] See Appendix 2 for a breakdown of the elements in the chronicle.

chronicle. Knighton added a date which is almost certainly wrong, and gives the area raided different dimensions. On the Lochmaben incident, both Knighton and the abbot of Meaux follow the short continuation account closely. In most details the short continuation tallies with the Lanercost chronicle, but the list of Scottish dead varies.[159] The Anonimalle manuscript itself omits the name of Bosco there, although his name is to be found in other texts of the short continuation.[160]

The original text of the short continuation seems to have ended about here, as shown above. Three manuscripts refer to the raid on Haddington (not in the Anonimalle manuscript), but none go on to record the battle of Halidon Hill, and it is therefore probable that this section and other information for 1333 and 1334 was composed at St Mary's itself.[161] This final section is equally interesting and valuable, although the dating and the battle positions pose problems. The initial date of 1334 for this part is clearly a slip since the events are simply continuations of those already correctly dated to 1333, and possibly reflects the compiler's recognition that he was starting a new section and using a new source. The dates for the arrival of Edward III at Berwick and the chronology of the assaults on the town, which many chroniclers report, remain uncertain. The Anonimalle narrative has Edward arrive on 16 May, but Dr Nicholson has established that Edward was already at Tweedmouth by 9 May. Perhaps 16 May was the first date on which Edward crossed the Tweed. The great attack on Berwick is dated here as 18 May, which fits quite well with the 20 May recorded in the Lanercost chronicle, and with those chronicles which write of a great assault as soon as Edward arrived. However, the Bridlington chronicler assumes the great assault to have been the immediate cause of the truces in early July, and Dr Nicholson, working back through the truces, suggested 27 June for the great assault. This account and that of Bridlington seem to be describing the same assault, with the burning of a church as its highlight, and a truce as a result, but the Anonimalle Chronicle puts the end of this first truce at 4 June. This date for the truce fits reasonably with its earlier

---

[159] *Knighton*, pp. 465–6; *Melsa*, pp. 367–8; 'Hemingburgh', p. 306; *Lanercost*, pp. 272–3.
[160] See for example Bodleian Library MS Lyell 17, fo. 121v. Knighton (p. 467), like the Anonimalle Chronicle, records only Jardine and Cardoil. The Meaux chronicle (p. 368) records Bosco and Jardine, but omits Cardoil, as does the Lanercost chronicle (p. 272).
[161] See p. 21.

chronology in May, but not at all with the known truces in
July. It is possible of course that over the period of the siege,
which all chroniclers agree was bitter, hard fought, and
damaging, there was more than one extra effort which could
be called a great assault, but it is also possible that the
Anonimalle's date of 4 June was a mistake for 4 July. Certainly
it assumes that the end of this first truce ran directly into the
eight-day truce which ended with the disputed relief of Berwick
on 11 July, and the hanging of Seton's son on 12 July. This
was followed by another truce until 19 July. Two eight day
truces, with the end of the first on 4 July, would fit with the
Bridlington chronicler's record of a fifteen day truce ending on
11 July, which might well have been made up of two of eight
days each. The long continuation of the *Brut* confirms an eight
day truce to 11 July.[162]

The best factual account on the English side of the actual
fighting at Halidon Hill is probably that of the canon of
Bridlington, which notes the battle divisions and commanders
of the English army, together with some of the Scots; the
Lanercost chronicle is shorter, but neatly describes the use of
English archers; the long continuation emphasises both the
archers and the dismounting of the knights.[163] However this
Anonimalle narrative has points of great interest. It contains
less on battle tactics, but offers a sensitive and no doubt justified
emphasis on the fears of the English and the comfort and
encouragement given by the young English king, and it
includes much detail on the Scottish army.

Points of greatest interest in the narrative are the detailed
lists of the leaders and numbers of the Scottish army, and the
insistence that the army was divided into four divisions instead
of the normal three. Only the long continuation of the *Brut*,
the continuator of 'Hemingburgh's' chronicle, and Knighton
have similarly lengthy lists, and of these only the first two
emphasise the four battle lines. Knighton redivides them into
the traditional three, although his lists of names retain the order
of the four divisions found in the 'Hemingburgh' continuator.
The only other chronicle to mention four divisions is that of
Meaux, but only when referring to the army which Douglas
first brought to Tweedmouth; it then reverts to a description

[162] Nicholson, op. cit., p. 117; *Lanercost*, p. 273; *Brid.*, pp. 111–14; *Melsa*, pp. 368–9; 'Hemingburgh',
pp. 307–8.
[163] *Brid.*, pp. 114–16; *Lanercost*, pp. 273–4; *Brut*, I, 283–6.

of three divisions for the battle of Halidon Hill.[164] When the lists of names are examined in detail, especially those in the long continuation, several sub-divisions appear within them, reflecting no doubt the practical tactics of the day: indeed the Bridlington chronicler notes wings and flanks of divisions in his account. It is, therefore, possible that the emphasis in these chronicles on four divisions is a faulty understanding of the tactics and organisation, with a subdivision counted as a separate unit. However it is equally possible, given the very precise nature of the lists and the details of their leaders, that the Scots did make an unusual disposition of their troops, which most chroniclers, being used to the descriptions of three divisions, failed to record. Certainly the dismounting of knights both here and at Dupplin Moor, shows current experiment in battle tactics,[165] and perhaps the account of four divisions should be taken as a further instance of experiment in unusual battle dispositions at this period.

The lists of names in these four detailed chronicles must come from a common source, as the accounts do not seem to be dependent on each other. The 'Hemingburgh' list is close to Knighton's, which is itself closer to the one in this account than to the list in the long continuation.[166] In this account the divisions are given as the first battle line, the 'my garde', the third, and fourth battle lines, with a supporting group from Berwick under Dunbar. The long continuation is more elaborate, giving the vanguard, the second battle line (divided into two), the third 'ward', and the fourth 'ward', with Dunbar's group described as the fifth 'ward' of the battle line. In Knighton's chronicle the first two battle lines (*acies*) are the same as the first two sections of the previous two chronicles; his third battle line (the 'rereward') is in fact the fourth section given in the other two. He adds to this, at the end, the names of those given in the third section of the other two, with no separate heading, yet this seems to be a separate section, beginning like the others with the names of the leading earls. Knighton has in fact retained the four sections of the other two but has rearranged them. He does not include Dunbar's group, but does list the absentees. The numbers of men in each section

---

[164] *Brut.*, I, 283–6; '*Hemingburgh*', pp. 308–9; *Knighton*, pp. 468–70; *Melsa*, pp. 369–70; Nicholson accepts the three divisions, op. cit., pp. 134–6.

[165] Nicholson, op. cit., pp. 133–4.

[166] See Appendix 3.

of the Anonimalle narrative and in the long continuation of the
Brut indicate four battle lines of roughly equal size. This account
provides in all 62 names, the long continuation has 68, Knighton
64, and the 'Hemingburgh' continuator only 32. At least 44
names are common to all lists, and this number might be higher
as spellings vary widely. This account does explain the incorrect
appearance of the infant earl of Mar in the long continuation's
list of those present at Halidon Hill, since in the third battle
line appears the name of David of Mar, whom the compiler of
the list in the long continuation clearly assumed to be the earl.

This account, like almost all the others, records the dead. It
gives more Scottish names (eight earls and twelve barons) than
elsewhere, yet only five of its earls are correct, because Moray
and Strathearn certainly and Menteith probably died at Dupplin
Moor. However, no other English chronicles were correct
either.[167] Numbers for the total Scottish dead are high in
all chronicles.[168] Undoubtedly, as after Dupplin Moor, an
exaggerated list of the Scottish losses was made. Such
exaggeration is not surprising since the Scots had greatly
outnumbered the English, and the sense of shock and disaster
on one side, and euphoria of victory on the other must have
been immense. The low estimate for the English losses is
common to all chronicles.[169]

The compiler at St Mary's continued to merge material up
to 1334, at which point he began to use a chronicle closely
related to that of Lanercost, but the section of the Anonimalle
Chronicle between this battle and the part already published
by Professor Galbraith is distinctly inferior to other sections. It
is an untidy compilation of the deaths of some religious, the
birth of a princess, and the homage of Balliol and Dunbar to
Edward III. The dating is superficially wrong because the
chronicler has already given the date 1334, although, as he
correctly says, all the episcopal deaths were in the same year as
Halidon Hill, that is 1333. Isabella was born in June 1332;
Jeanne was born in late 1333, but in the Tower. Other chronicles
show how the mistake might arise.[170] Then the death of Pope

---

[167] *Lanercost*, p. 274, correctly names four earls but wrongly records that seven were killed;
Knighton, p. 468, names six; *Brid.*, p. 116, wrongly records seven killed without naming them.
[168] They vary from lower figures of 35,712 and 36,320 to an upper one of 90,000 for those both
killed and who fled; Nicholson, op. cit., p. 137; *Brut*, I, 286; *Lanercost*, p. 274; *Murimuth*, p. 68.
[169] See for instance *Brut*, I, 286; *Brid.*, p. 116; *Melsa*, p. 370.
[170] See *Murimuth*, pp. 71–2; *Ann. Paul.*, p. 361; *Le Baker*, p. 53, which show how the mistake
could have evolved.

John XXII, and the homage of Balliol and Dunbar are wrongly placed in 1333. There is a simple miscopying of the year dates here, but Balliol's homage is placed two days too late. In the subsequent sentences, already published by Professor Galbraith, the chronicle continues to show an untidy merging of sources: it repeats Dunbar's surrender of Berwick, and repeats the death of the pope (this time under 1335). It then returns to correct dating with the next Scottish affairs as it draws on its version of the Lanercost chronicle.

Despite its occasional dating errors, and one or two confused passages, especially towards the end when sources are being merged, the Anonimalle narrative for these years is an interesting one. In its final Scottish section it provides details not found in other chronicles, and its description of the battle at Halidon Hill is worth further study. Perhaps even more importantly it preserves the fullest version of the short continuation of the French prose *Brut*, the value of which is already acknowledged by historians. As mentioned above, it was a popular chronicle, both reflecting and moulding views of the reign of Edward II and the early years of Edward III, and was used as a trustworthy source not only in the *Croniques de London*, but also by later compilers such as Knighton and the abbot of Meaux. It offers us unique details, particularly but not exclusively on London affairs, on the Marchers' movements in 1321–2, and in early Scottish affairs. Throughout, it is presented as a factual and sensible account of events, and the author, quite possibly a government clerk, is, in the main, reliable. Where he cites documents directly he does so accurately; in several passages he also shows himself familiar with the content and essential points of others; in passages such as those on the rebellion of Lancaster or the fall of Mortimer he shows himself a concise, competent, and informed political commentator. Some of the errors seen in this text have clearly crept in at some point through faulty copying. The relationships of the Anonimalle text and the various versions of the short continuation are complex, and there is much room for further study of these, as well as of the relationships between the short continuation and other chroniclers who borrowed from it.

Appendix 1

The use of the short continuation as a contemporary source

As mentioned in the introduction to the text one indication of the importance of the *Brut* continuation lies in the use made of it by a number of fourteenth-century chroniclers. Within a decade of its compilation passages from its text were transcribed in the *Croniqes de London*. Later in the century both the Meaux chronicler, Thomas Burton, and Henry Knighton at St Mary's, Leicester, used its narrative. The continuation was probably known also to the author of the *Historia Aurea*, who quoted Isabella's letter to the city of London, found only in the fullest versions of the text. It is also possible that its narrative was used by the author of the *Gesta Edwardi de Carnarvan*, although the precise relationship between the two narratives is difficult to establish.[1]

Undoubtedly the greatest use of the short continuation is found in the *Croniques de London*, written during the middle years of the fourteenth century. In its account of Edward II's reign the *Croniques* quotes the text of this continuation on several occasions. The use by a London chronicler of the short continuation as a source both for national and London history reinforces the impression that the continuation had London associations. Below are listed those passages in the *Croniques de London* which appear to derive wholly or in part from the fullest version of the short continuation as found in the Anonimalle text. These passages occur mainly between 1312 and 1327. It is worth noting that as a source primarily concerned with London history the *Croniques* did not use the *Brut*'s northern narrative.

Passages from the *Croniques de London* which appear to be taken from the *Brut* continuation include:

1312   A phrase on the execution of Gaveston (p. 36).
1315   The account of the spire at St Pauls (p. 38).
1321   The siege of Leeds Castle (pp. 42–3).

---

[1] See pp. 63–4.

1322	The executions after Boroughbridge (there are slight similarities) (p. 44). London forces sent to the king at Newcastle (pp. 44–5). The account of the two Mortimers (p. 45).
1323	The account of Andrew Harclay (there are slight similarities) (p. 45). Hamo de Chigwell (pp. 45–6). The miracles associated with Thomas of Lancaster (p. 46).
1324	Thomas Newbiggin and the Mortimers (p. 47). Discord between the kings of France and England (p. 48).
1326	The king forbids letters to be carried from the queen (p. 49). Fires on account of the drought (p. 50). French merchants forbidden to come to England (p. 50). The queen's forces in France (pp. 50–1). Isabella lands in Essex (p. 51). The Anonimalle continuation locates Harwich as in Suffolk. Isabella's letters to the city of London (p. 51). The text of the second letter is not given. The king flees to Bristol (p. 55). The fate of Despenser and others (pp. 56–7).
1327	Isabella and Edward hold a parliament (p. 57). The proclamation in Cheapside (p. 57). Thomas Dunheved and Edward II (p. 58). Franchises granted to London (p. 59).

The relationship between the short continuation and the compilation known as the *Gesta Edwardi de Carnarvan*, written by a canon of Bridlington, is not entirely clear. What is certain is that primarily in the section from 1328 to 1334 the two narratives contain entries of a similar character. These include notices of the marriage of Edward III, the coronation of the queen, the birth of the king's son, the homage for Gascony (placed under 1329 in the *Gesta*), and the accident at the Cheapside tournament.[2] In the two chronicles the sequence of events after 1328 is similar. Both contain an expanded account

---

[2] *Brid.* pp. 99, 100, 101, 102. See pp. 138, 142, 144, 146.

of the Anglo-Scottish campaigns of 1332–3, and under 1334 both mention the Durham episcopal elections followed by an entry on Balliol's homage to Edward III.[3] Brief entries in the Edward II section of the *Gesta* referring to episcopal elections in 1316, 1320, and 1321 are also similar to entries in the *Brut* continuation.[4] The closest correspondence occurs in the account of Louis of Bavaria's election of Nicholas V as anti-pope in 1328.[5] In this passage the wording of the two accounts is almost identical, although the *Brut* continuation dates the event to 1327, and the canon of Bridlington to 1329. Because the entry appears to be an interpolation in the text of the *Brut* continuation a first impression might suggest that the St Mary's chronicler took this passage from the *Gesta*. It is possible, however, that both accounts were indebted to a common source.[6] In addition to the passage on Nicholas V several entries which are common to the two accounts appear to be interpolations in the *Brut* text. They may derive from a set of contemporary annals which circulated in the York diocese, and which were known to both the Anonimalle chronicler and the author of the *Gesta*. It is, however, just possible that the Anonimalle chronicler used an early draft of the *Gesta*, already in existence when the Anonimalle manuscript was being compiled.[7]

The later use of the *Brut* continuation is more obvious. At the end of the century the Meaux chronicler, Thomas Burton, used the short continuation of the *Brut* as one source for the retrospective section of his history. As a text with northern associations, a copy of the continuation is likely to have been in the Meaux library.[8] Thus under 1314 the chronicler's notice of the prices ordinance appears to owe something to this continuation.[9] His description of the Despensers is similar to the account found in the *Brut*, but is placed under 1320, and not *c.* 1317–18 as in the *Brut* text.[10] The account of the exile of the Despensers is again similar, as is the description of the siege

[3] *Brid.* pp. 111–19. See pp. 158–70.
[4] *Brid.* pp. 49, 60, 61. See pp. 90, 98, 100.
[5] *Brid.* pp. 100–1. See pp. 134, 136.
[6] The account of the election of Nicholas V is part of a longer passage in the continuation, the whole of which appears to have a Franciscan interest. See p. 19.
[7] In the form in which it survives the *Gesta* was composed late in Edward III's reign, but it appears to be based upon an earlier text which originally extended to 1339.
[8] See *Kirkstall Abbey Chronicles* (Thoresby Society, 1952), p. 9.
[9] *Melsa*, II, 332.
[10] Ibid. II, 337–8.

of Leeds Castle.[11] A passage on London forces sent to the aid of the king almost certainly derives from this continuation, as does the account of the imprisonment of the Mortimers.[12] The description in the Meaux chronicle of the fires at Royston, Croxton, and Wandlesworth almost certainly comes from the short continuation.[13] Similarly the account of the letter to the Londoners in 1326 appears to derive from the short continuation, although the text of the letter is not given.[14] The Meaux chronicle is also indebted to the short continuation for its account of the campaigns of 1332 and 1333. It has similarities with the continuation both as regards its description of the siege of Berwick, and the battle of Halidon Hill. The Meaux chronicle does not, however, preserve the list of names in the battle formations of the Scots, and from its general information it is clear that the chronicler must have used other sources as well as the *Brut* continuation for this part of the narrative.[15]

Like the Meaux chronicler, Henry Knighton of St Mary's, Leicester, wrote at the end of the century. He first began work in the 1380s on the later part of his chronicle (1377–95), and subsequently wrote the earlier section of his narrative which extended from 1066 to 1366.[16] In this early section Knighton's text is indebted to the *Polychronicon (Cistrensis)*, and to a number of sources which he collectively described as *Leycestrensis*. These sources await detailed analysis, but among them, possibly incorporated in a text of Walter of Guisborough, was the short continuation of the *Brut*. Knighton used the text of the continuation for his account of the Anglo-Scottish campaigns of 1332–3, illustrating again the value placed on this part of the *Brut* narrative.[17] Elsewhere he quoted from the *Brut*'s narrative in his description of the execution of the earl of Kent.[18]

[11] Ibid. II, 338–40.
[12] Ibid. II, 340, 341, 345. See pp. 42–3.
[13] Ibid. II, 349.
[14] Ibid. II, 351.
[15] Ibid. II, 362–5, 367–8.
[16] V. H. Galbraith, 'The Chronicle of Henry Knighton', in D. J. Gordon (ed.) *Fritz Saxl 1890–1948. A Volume of Memorial Essays* (London, 1957).
[17] *Knighton*, I, 461–6. For an English chronicler Knighton has a pronounced interest in Anglo-Scottish affairs. Professor A. A. M. Duncan has pointed out that Knighton was concerned later with the question of David II's release from captivity.
[18] *Knighton*, I, 452.

Appendix 2

The Roxburgh and Annandale raids

The Anonimalle text seems to be at its most confused in narrating these episodes. Its information becomes clearer if the narrative is broken up into its constituent parts and is then re-ordered.

Present narrative

A   Puis le dit monsire Edward de Baillol ove sez gentz qil avoit sen ala a Rokesburgh et la demura une piece

B   Le counte Patrik et Archebaud Douglas et autres grantz Descoce qi furent demurez en vie maunderent a sire Edward de Baillol qi adonqe fu fait roi Descoz . . . et le roi meismes a grante peine sen fuist oue autrement il eust este trahi

C   Mes sire Thomas Vghtred qi adonqe estoit noble chivaler et vaillant od dis hommes darmes tauntsoulement (fo. 267) combatirent . . . et illueqe fu pris Andreu de Moret et altres

D   Meis Johan Crabbe od grante peine eschapa et dolerousement sen fuist a Berewyk et la se tint

E   Denapres sire Edward de Baillol entra la terre Descoz od les grantz seignurs Dengleterre et od lour gentz le samady en la semaine de quaresme . . . pris une peel en le quel ils troverent monsire Robert de Colvill . . . puis sen alerent a Berewyk . . . (fo. 267v) ils lesserent lour sege et se remuerent dillueqe et vindrent en Engleterre.

F   En cel temps le roi tint son parlement a Everwyk . . . les gentz Descoz qi touz jours furent faux et compassantz de mal, vindrent a sire Edward de Baillof et autrefoiz li prierent de enduces . . . meis avint issint al aide de dieu qe plusours grantz seignurs de la partie Descoz furent illuqe occis cestassaver sire Johan de Moubray Descoz, sire Walter Comyn, sire William de la Beche, sire Johan Talebot et plusours autres

G   Et le roi Descoce avoit la victoire

H   Lan Mille CCCXXXIII plusours grauntz seignurs Dengleterre revindrent a Berewyk et autrefoicz assegerent la ville . . .

Re-ordered narrative

A better, although still not perfect order, would seem to be:

A   The arrival at Roxburgh.

C   Ughtred's fight at the bridge (the opening sentences of the attack appear to have been omitted and the beginning of the Annandale raid copied instead).

D   Crabbe's escape (the wording comes from his earlier escape at the siege of Perth).

G   The victory was Balliol's.

F, B   Some leave for parliament; Dunbar and Douglas ask for a truce; the Annandale attack; the king's flight to England.

E   Balliol and some English lords come to Berwick, taking Colville's peel on the way.

H   Some English lords try to persuade Berwick to surrender to Edward III rather than to Balliol.

The chronology of the raids in Gilsland and on Lochmaben, and the arrival of Edward III in Scotland are then in the correct order.

Appendix 3

A comparison of the Scots at Halidon Hill as recorded in the four most detailed chronicles

Anonimalle manuscript[*]	*Long continuation*[†]	*Knighton*[‡]	*Continuation of 'Hemingburgh'* [§]
In quatre batailles	in iiii wenges	in tribus aciebus	quatuor acies disposuerunt
LA PRIMERE BATAILLE	THE VANT-WARD OF SCOTLAND	IN PRIMA ACIE	IN PRIMA (ACIE)
Counte de Mouref	Erl of Morrif	Comes de Moryf	Comes Moraviae
James Fryselle	Iames Friselle	Jacobus Frysell	Jacobus Frisel
Symond Fryselle	Symond Friselle	Symon Frysell	Simon Frisel
Walter Stiward	Walter Stiward	Walterus Styward	Walterus Steward
Reynald Cleyme	Raynolde Cheyne	Reginaldus Clene	Reginaldus de Chene
Patrik de Graham	Patrik of Graham	Patrik de Grahamseneth	Patricius de Grame
Johan Graunde	Iohn le Graunt	Johannes Grant	Johannes Graunt
James de Cardoille	Iames of Cardoile	Johannes de Carlyl	Johannes de Bardale
Patrik de Chartris	Patrik Parkeres	Patricius Careter	Patricius de Berechere
Robert de Caldecotes	Robert Caldecotes	Robertus de Caldecote	Robertus de Caldecotes
Philippe Mildroun	Philip of Meldrum	Patricius de Meldrome	Phillipus de Meldrom
William Hardyn	—	Willelmus Gareyne	Willelmus 'de Gardin'
Thomas Cherpatrik	Thomas —	Thomas Toker	Thomas de Kyrkpatrik
Gilbert Wysman	Gilbert Wiseman	Gylbertus Wysman	Gilbertus Wiseman
Adam Burdoun	Adam Gurdoun	Adam de Cordon	Adam Gordun

[*] Below pp. 164–6.
[†] *Brut*, I, 283–5.
[‡] *Knighton*, pp. 468–70.
[§] *'Hemingburgh'*, pp. 308–9.

John de Burgh	—	—	Willelmus 'Gordoun'
James de Graveuasch	Iamys Gramat	Jacobus Granegranche	Jacobus Garnegarth
Johan Grandels le ficz	—	Alanus Graunte	Alanus Graunt
Robert Barde	Robert Boyde	Robertus Boyth	Robertus Boid
—	Hughe Park	—	—
600 hommes darmes	600 men of armes	300 viri armati	300 armatorum
14,200 de la commune	3,000 of commune	2,200 communes	2,200 de communitate leviter armati
40 bachilers	40 knyztes newe dobbede	—	—

EN LA MY GARDE	FERST PARTIE OF THE HALFE BATAILE OF SCOTLAND	IN SECUNDA ACIE	IN SECUNDA ACIE
Seneschalle Descoce, counte de Meneth	Styward of Scotland, Erl of Moneteth	Senescallus Scotiae	Senescallus Scotiae
James son uncle	Iames his Uncle	Jacobus avunculus eius	Jacobus avunculus suus
(see below)	(see below)	Maclinus filius Andensis	Malcolmus Fleming
William Douglas	William Douglas	Willelmus Douglas filius Jacobi Duglas	Willelmus Douglas filius Jacobi Douglas
Johan le ficz Johan de Galeway	—	—	—
David de Lindesey	David of Lyndeseye	David de Lyndeshey	David de Lyndesey
Maucoloun Flemyng	Maucolyn Flemyng	(see above)	(see above)
William de Keth	William of Keth	—	Willelmus de Keth marescallus exercitus
David Kambel	Dunkan Kambok	Duncanus Cambell	Dunecanus de Cambel
—	30 bachilers new dobbede	—	Plures quam 11 milites

	SECUNDE PART OF THE HALF LIEN-WARDE OF THE BATAILE OF SCOTLAND		
James Stiward de Aldyngtoun	Iames Stiward of Colden	Jacobus Styward de Daldon	—
Johan de Burgh	—	—	—
Aleine Stiward (see Hirchyn)	Aleyne Styward	Adam Styward	—
	—	Willelmus Yriskin	—
William de Aberconeweye	—	Willelmus Abrenythy	—
William Hirchyn	—	(see Yriskin)	—
William Albertyn	William Abbrehyn	—	—
William de Morref le ficz	William Morice	Willelmus Moresth	—
John le ficz sire William	Iohn fitz William	—	—
Adam de Murref de Layntoun	Adam le Mose	—	—
Johan de Shirestoun	—	—	—
—	Walter fitz Gilbert	Walterus fitz Gilbert	—
—	Iohn of Cherlton	Johannes de Grettone	—
—	Robert Walham	—	—
—	—	Willelmus Moresth de Glawlton	—
700 hommes darmes	700 men of armes	300 viris bene armatis	300 armatis
17,000 de la commune	17,000 of communes	300 de communibus armatis	3,000 de communitate leviter armatorum
LA TERCE BATAILLE	THRIDDE WARD OF THE BATAILE OF SCOTLAND	CUM. . .¶	IN QUARTA ACIE¶
—	Erl of Marr	—	—

¶ In *Knighton* and 'Hemingburgh' the groups which were placed third in the Anonimalle Chronicle and in the long continuation were placed fourth. They are reversed here for ease of comparison.

counte de Roos	Erl of Roff	comite de Rosse	comites de Ros
counte de Shornlond	Erl of Straherne	comite de Southlande	de Sonderland
counte de Straverne	Erle of Sotherland	comite de Stratherne	de Stretherne
Walter de Chilteleye	William Kirkeleye	Walterus de Kyrkeby	—
Johan Cambron	Iohn Cambron	Johannes de Cambron	—
Gilbert de la Haye	Gilbert de Haye	Gilbertus de Saye	—
David de Mar	—	David de Marre	—
—	William of Rameseye	—	—
—	William Proudegest	—	—
Griffyn de la Harde	Kirstyn Hard	Cristinus de Harde	—
Johan Brounynge	—	filius de Bremmyng	—
—	William Gurdon	—	—
—	Arnolde Garde	—	—
—	Thomas Dolfyn	—	—
—	—	Oliverus de seint Clere	Plures quam 12 milites
900 hommes darmes	900 men of armes	200 viris armatis	200 armatis
15,000 de la commune	15,000 of communes	4,000 de communibus armatis	4,000 de communitate leviter armati
30 bachilers	40 knyghtes new dobbede	—	—

LA QUATRE BATAILLE	FERTHE WARDE OF THE BATAILE OF SCOTLAND	IN TERCIA ACIE SCILICET LE REREWARDE¶	IN TERCIA ACIE¶
—	—	Comes de Carryk	Dominus de Carich
Archebaud Douglas	Archebald Douglas	Archibaldus Douglas	Archebaudus Douglas
—	—	Alexander Larneys	—
Counte de Levenax	Erl of Leneux	Comes de Kenenanz	Comes de Levenax

Alisaundre de Roos seigneur de Laverne	Alisaunder le Brus	—	Alexander Brus
Counte de Fif	Erl of Fiff	Comes de Fyth	—
Johan Cambel qe se cleyme counte Dathels	Iohn Cambel, Erl of Atheles	Johannes Clavelle qi se clamat comitem de Asseles	Johannes Cambel
Robert Loweder, ficz	Robert Lawether	Robert le Wyther filius	—
(see below)	(see below)	Jocus de Scherlynghong	—
William de Wippount	William Vipount	Willelmus de Veson	—
William de Hingestoun	William of Lonston	Willelmus de Lyngiston	—
Johan de Landels	Iohn de Labelles	—	—
Joce de Semperlowe	Gros de Sherenlowe	(see above)	—
William Frisel	(see below)	(see below)	—
Johan de Lindeseye de Walpole	Iohn of Lyndeseye	Johannes de Lyndesleye	—
(see above)	(see above)	Willelmus de Frysleye	—
—	—	Bernardus Frysell	—
—	—	Alexander de Lyndesleye	—
Alisaundre de Grey	Alisaunder de Gray	Alexander de Gray	—
—	Ingam de Umfreuil	Willelmus de Umfranwe	—
—	Patrik de Pollesworth	Patricius de Yleward	—
—	David de Wymes	David de Wymes	—
—	Michel Scott	Willelmus Scot	—
—	William Landy	Willelmus de Land	—
Thomas de Bois	Thomas de Boys	(see below)	—
Roger le Mortumer	Rogere de Mortymer	Rogerus de Mortemer	—
(see above)	(see above)	Thomas de Veys	—

		Willelmus de Cambowe	et plures quam 17 milites
900 hommes darmes	900 men of armes	300 armatis de communibus armatis	300 armatis
18,000 de la commune	18,000 communes	—	4,300 de communitate leviter armati
80 bachilers	30 bachilers	—	—
(ALSO)	V^{TE} WARDE OF THE BATAILE OF SCOTLAND		
Patrik de Dunbar	Erl of Dunbarre	—	—
50 hommes darmes	50 men of armes	—	—
la commune de la ville sanz nombre	—	—	—
—	Alisaundre of Seton	—	—
—	100 men of armes	—	—
—	the comons of the toun with 400 men of armes	—	—
—	10,800 of fotemen	—	—
		Not present	
—	—	Alexander de Miners	—
—	—	Willelmus de Prendersoit	—
—	—	Robertus de Condre, pater	—
—	—	Robertus de Keth	—
—	—	Edwardus de Keth	—
—	—	Patricius de Brythyne	—

Appendix 4

Provisional List of Manuscripts containing the short *Brut* continuation

MSS	Provenance	Date
Cambridge		
Cambridge University Library		
Gg.1.15.		XIV Cent.
Mm.1.33.		XIV Cent?
Trinity College		
R.5.32	(contains Avesbury)	XV Cent.
R.7.14	Seneschal of count of Weedon Beck	XIV Cent.
Dublin		
Trinity College		
500 (formerly E.2.33)	London, St John of Jerusalem	XIV Cent.
Edinburgh		
University Library		
181		XIV Cent.
Leeds		
Brotherton Library		
MS 29	St Mary's, York (Anonimalle Chronicle)	XIV Cent.
London		
British Library		
Add. 18462	Sir Simonds D'Ewes (fragment)	XV Cent.
35113		XIV Cent.
Cleopatra D.VII		XIV Cent.
Cotton Julius A.VI	Manuscript contains Pipewell material (fragment)	XIV Cent.
Domitian A.X		XIV Cent.
Harley 200	Sir Simonds D'Ewes (contains Avesbury)	XV Cent.
6359	Sir Simonds D'Ewes?	XIV Cent.
College of Arms		
Arundel 31		XIV Cent.
Inner Temple		
Petyt 511		XIV Cent.

Lambeth Library
504   XIV Cent.
Westminster Abbey
25   XIV Cent.
Oxford
  Bodleian Library

Douce 128	(contains Avesbury)	XV Cent.
Lyell 17	St Mary's, York	XIV Cent.
Rawlinson 329		XIV Cent.

Paris
  Bibliothèque de
  l'Arsenal
  3346   XV Cent.
  Bibliothèque Nationale
  12156   XV Cent.

Note on Editorial Method

The text

1. The text has been transcribed as written, retaining all original spelling, including those spellings which appear to be minor slips (for example Oxenfod, chauneller, Caernavan, vengeane, ville and velle for veille, wille for ville). Where omission of abbreviation marks has affected spelling, necessary letters have been supplied in editorial brackets (Richmu[n]d). Deletions and insertions in the text are indicated in round brackets. Necessary editorial corrections to errors in the text are indicated within square brackets. Editorial comment is provided in italics within the brackets. In several places where there are clearly omissions in the text, in order to make sense of a passage a few words have been supplied, given in round brackets, from Bodleian MS Lyell 17 or Cambridge University Library MS Mm.1.33. The source of each addition has been indicated in a footnote. Six marginal notes in the text in a late medieval hand have also been indicated by footnotes, but lesser marginalia, mostly the word *nota* in a red box, have not been shown.

2. Capital letters have been retained only for proper names.

3. The text is profusely but inconsistently punctuated. Punctuation has therefore been simplified, while being kept as close as possible to the text.

4. Paragraph divisions are the editors'.

5. Abbreviations have been extended: *oū* has been printed as *oun* or *oum*, *q̄* as *qe*, and *qz* has also been printed as *qe*, although some words show the variety possible (*illueqe, illueqes*). *Plu'* and *su'* have been printed as *plus* and *sus*. The letters *u* and *v*, *i* and *j* have been printed according to modern usage.

6. Certain passages appear to have been added to the *Brut* continuation in this text. Those passages which can be confidently identified as interpolations have been printed here in italics. They refer to Franciscan and Yorkshire history, episcopal appointments, and to extracts which derive from the short Latin chronicle on the opening folios (fos. 26v–29) of the Anonimalle manuscript.

The translation

1. The style reflects as closely as possible the form of the text, although some changes have been necessary to provide readable modern English.

2. Punctuation and sentence division are those of the editors.

3. All proper names, Christian names, and surnames have been modernised where the modern equivalent is known.

4. *Grauntz* has been translated throughout as lords and *monsire* and *sire* as sir, in conformity with the usages indicated in the fourteenth-century English translation of the long continuation of the *Brut*.

5. Modern dates have been inserted in the translation by the editors in square brackets.

THE ANONIMALLE CHRONICLE
1307 to 1334

Text

The Anonimalle Chronicle, 1307–1334

(fo. 248v)

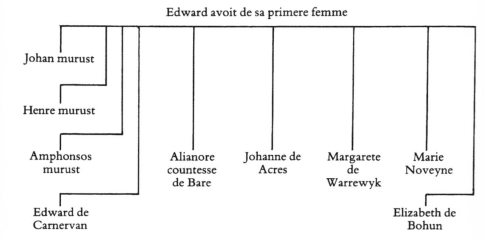

Edward avoit de sa primere femme

Johan murust

Henre murust

Amphonsos murust | Alianore countesse de Bare | Johanne de Acres | Margarete de Warrewyk | Marie Noveyne

Edward de Carnervan | | | | Elizabeth de Bohun

Edward de Caernervan

Apres cestui bone roi Edward regna Edward son ficz. Edward de Carnervan fust appelle, beaus homme et fort de corps et de membre, mes il forslisna de les tetches et de la manere son pere, qar il ne fist force de chivalerie ne pruesce, mes tantsoullement de sa volente demene. Cestui roi Edward fu si chaungeable de corage et de quoer, qe ceo qil granta une jour pur commun profist de la terre il le voleit dedir une autre jour. Et auxi fust il homme de grante vengeance, qar quant il comenca (de: *deleted*) de regner tost apres grande descord et grande estrif sourdirent entre li et une sire Walter de Langetoun, qi fust evesqe de Cestre et tresorere le roi son pere, pur ceo qe le dit evesqe li accusa quant il estoit prince de Gales dascunes trespas et meffaitz, des queux le bone roi son pere li reprova et chastia par droit et reson. Cesti roi aima cherement de coer ascuns gentz qi son piere sovent foith li defendi la compaignie de eux, come une sire Peres

The Anonimalle Chronicle, 1307–1334

(fo. 248v)

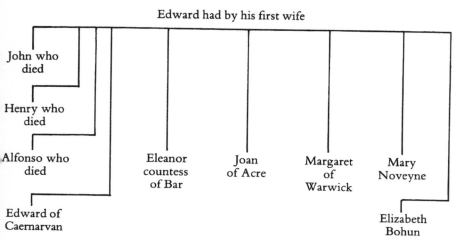

Edward had by his first wife

John who died

Henry who died

Alfonso who died

Edward of Caernarvan

Eleanor countess of Bar

Joan of Acre

Margaret of Warwick

Mary Noveyne

Elizabeth Bohun

Edward of Caernarvan

After this good king, Edward, his son Edward reigned. He was called Edward of Caernarvan, a handsome man and strong in body and limb, but he fell short of the qualities and the style of his father, for he was concerned not with deeds of chivalry or prowess but only with his own desires. This king Edward was so fickle in purpose and feelings that what he granted one day for the common profit of the land he would want to retract on another. Also he was a man bent on vengeance, for soon after he began to reign great discord and conflict arose between himself and a certain sir Walter Langton, who was bishop of Chester [Coventry and Lichfield] and had been treasurer of the king, his father, because the said bishop had accused him, when he was prince of Wales, of various evil deeds and wrongdoings for which the good king, his father, had reproved and rightly and reasonably punished him. This king loved with all his heart certain people whose company his father had frequently forbidden him, among them a certain sir Piers

(fo. 249)

de Gavastoun qi fust par le bone roi son pere exile, et par les
bons pers de la terre, meis cel exil ne dura gueres, qar tost
apres, meisme cel an qil fu coroune, il fist remander le dit Pers
encountre la defense son pere et sanz assent de son barnage a
lui dona le counte (de counte: *deleted in red*) de Cornewaille, et
li fist counte. *Et auxint il li dona a femme sa nece la fille monsire
Gilbert de Clare counte de Gloucestre et dame Johanne de Acres soer a
meisme celi roi Dengleterre.* Cesti roi dehonura les bones gentz de
sa terre et honura les enemis, come flatours, mauconseilers et
meffesours, qi li conseillerent encountre sa coroune et encontre
commun (profit)[1] de la terre et les tint assetz chier, come par
my sez faitz serra plus pleinement dist apres.

   Lan Mille CCCVII le roi Edward passa le xxij jour de Janver
la meer, et esposa dame Isabelle la fille le roi de Fraunce a
Boloigne de sur la meer ove grand joie et od grand honur. Et la
primere anne de son regne furent ils corounez a Westminstre
od grant solempnite et od grant honur del evesqe de Wincestre
(et: *interlined*) dautres evesqes, le ix kalend de Marcz,[2] qe fu le
dimanche lendemain de la feste de seint Piere in cathidra, qe
adonqe fu le dimanche de quaresme pernant, lan de grace
avantdit. *Et en cel temps jeust Robert ercevesqe de Caunterbury
malades, par quei il ne poeit estre a cel corounement.* Meisme cel an
furent les templers destruitz et anientez. Meisme cel an le roi et
le dit sire Piers, le counte de Garenne pristrent lour chimin vers
Escoz apres la feste de seint Michil, et la demurerent tut le yver
ensuant.

   Lan Mille CCCVIII le barnage de la terre voleient amendre
et redrescer plousours defautes, mespressiouns et grevaunces,
qe furent faitz par le roi et ses malveis counseillours, des queux
le poeple mult se pleinent, et assemblerent trestutz a Loundres
et illueqes monstrerent au roi lour grevances et lui prierent qils
purroient ordener teles ordinances sur les dites defautes,
mespressiouns et grevances qe serroient al honure de dieu et de
seint eglise et al honure du roi et profist de lui et de son roialme,
et le roi les granta franchement et de bone volunte,

---

[1] Bodleian Library MS Lyell 17, fo. 112.
[2] Coronation day, 25 February, was indeed the Sunday after St Peter in Cathedra, and the Sunday
before Lent, but it was not 9 but 6 kal Mar. in 1308 (a leap year).

(fo. 249)

Gaveston who had been exiled by the good king his father and by the good peers of the land; but his exile scarcely lasted any time, for soon after, in the same year that he was crowned, he had the said Piers recalled against his father's prohibition and without the consent of his baronage, and gave him the earldom of Cornwall, and made him an earl. And he also gave him for his wife his niece, the daughter of sir Gilbert de Clare, earl of Gloucester, and of lady Joan of Acre, sister of this same king of England. This king dishonoured the good people of his land and honoured its enemies, such as flatterers, false counsellors and wrongdoers, who gave him advice contrary to his royal estate and the common (profit) of the land, and he held them very dear as will be more fully related among his deeds hereafter.

In 1307 king Edward crossed the sea on 22 January [1308], and married lady Isabella, the daughter of the king of France, at Boulogne-sur-Mer, amid great joy and great honour. And in the first year of his reign they were crowned at Westminster with great solemnity and great ceremony by the bishop of Winchester and other bishops, on the ninth day before the kalends of March, which was the Sunday following the feast of St Peter in Cathedra, which was then the Sunday before Lent [25 February],[3] in the year of grace aforesaid. At this time Robert, archbishop of Canterbury, was ill so that he was not able to be present at the coronation. In the same year the Templars were destroyed and eliminated. In the same year the king and the said sir Piers, [and] earl Warenne made their way to Scotland after the feast of Michaelmas [29 September, 1310], and stayed there all the following winter.

In 1308 the baronage of the land wished to put right and make good several of the failures, misdeeds, and wrongs which had been committed by the king and his evil counsellors, of whom the people were greatly complaining. They all assembled at London and there they set forth their injuries to the king and begged him that they might be allowed to make such ordinances relating to the same failures, misdeeds and wrongs as should be to the honour of God and the Holy Church and to the honour of the king and to the profit of himself and his kingdom; and the king granted these requests freely and with a good will,

[3] See text, note 2.

(fo. 249v)

et lour dona sa commission enseale de souz son grant seal. Et les plus loiaux et les plus sages des prelatz, countez, barouns, et altres grantz de la terre feurent tittles par commun assent de faire les dites ordinances, par vertu de quele commission ils avoient ordenez divers pointz bones et covenables pur profit du roi et de tut le roialme, les queux pointz feurent desputez, examinez et triez devant le roi et son conseille, et le roi les avoit bien entendu, et charge qe les agrea, accepta, ratifia, et par son seal les conferma, et les delivera a sire Thomas de Tuttebury, adonqe counte de Lancastre et seneschal Dengleterre, et a tut le barnage de la terre. Et a la croice del cimter de seint Poel de Loundres feurent les dites ordinances publiez et proclamez, et ceux de Loundres avoient la copie dez dites ordinances desouz le grant seal le roi, et altres citees et burghs par my la terre. (Et de chescune cite et burgh par my la terre: *deleted in red*). Et de chescune citee et burgh par my la terre feurent gentz jurrez a Loundres, sur la croice lercevesqe de Caunterbury Robert de Wynchelse, et aux touz les graunz de la terre jurerent de sauvement garder et maintenere les ditz ordinances, et qi qe les enfreindroit seroit destruite et malmis. En les queles ordinances fust une point ordene, qe touz les malveis conseillers le roi seroient oustez et remuez du roi, par qei le dit Piers de Gavastoun, qestoit en temps le pere de cesti roi exile pur diverses enchesouns, et repelli par meismes cesti roi come de sus est dit, (qil: *interlined*) counseilla altrement le roi qe faire ne dust, encountre lestat de lui et de sa corone, et fist ensealer blaunches chartres et altres feitz nient covennables, si come les prelatz et les pers de la terre monstrerent grevousement par lor ordinaunces et examinementz faitz encontre lui, par qei il fust autrefoicz exile de la terre, et il sen ala en Flaundres a la fest de Touz Seintz et la se tint une pece. *Mais il dota le roi de Fraunce, par qei il revint en Engleterre en tour le Noel apres, et le roi lui recesceut joiousement* encontre les ordinances par lui et son conseil faitz, et li retint ove lui et li maintenist en sa compaignie encontre touz entre clamantz.

Lan Mille CCCXII en la feste

(fo. 249v)

and gave them his commission sealed with his great seal. The most loyal and wise of the prelates, earls, barons, and other lords of the land were authorised by common assent to make the same Ordinances. By virtue of this commission they made various good and suitable clauses for the profit of the king and the whole of the kingdom. These clauses were discussed, examined and settled before the king and his council; the king had understood them perfectly well, and declared that he was satisfied with them, accepted and ratified them, and confirmed them with his seal, and handed them over to sir Thomas of Tutbury, then earl of Lancaster and the steward of England, and to all the baronage of the land. The said Ordinances were publicised and proclaimed at the cross in the cemetery of St Paul's in London, and the Londoners and other cities and boroughs throughout the land had a copy of the said Ordinances under the king's great seal. And people from each city and borough throughout the country were sworn at London on the cross of the archbishop of Canterbury, Robert Winchelsey, and also all the lords of the land swore to guard safely and uphold the said Ordinances, and that whoever should infringe them would be destroyed and brought to harm. In the said Ordinances one point was made to the effect that all the evil counsellors of the king should be removed and dismissed from the king. Because of this, the said Piers Gaveston, who had been exiled for various reasons in the time of this king's father, and who had been recalled by this same king as is described above, was again exiled from the country, because he advised the king to do otherwise than he should, against his own estate and that of his crown, and because he caused blank charters to be sealed, and did other totally wrong things, as the prelates and the peers of the land demonstrated in an aggrieved manner through their Ordinances and investigations made against him. He went to Flanders on the feast of All Saints [1 November, 1311], and stayed there a while; but he feared the king of France, wherefore he returned to England about the following Christmas; and the king received him joyfully despite the Ordinances made by himself and his council, and kept him with him and in his company in the face of all protests.

In 1312 on the feast of

(fo. 250)

de seint Johan devant porte Latyn, fu termine a Vienne le conseil le
pape, en quel conseil lordre des templers fut destruit. En meisme
cel an les grantz de la terre porsiwerent quointement et
enginousement le dit sire Piers de Gavastoun, issint qen tour la
feste de seint Botolf le dit sire Piers vint a Dadygtoun prede
Oxenford, et le countee de Warrewyk lui prist a force, et
lamena al chastel de Elmele, et dillueqe tanqe a Warrewyk oue
il fust juge par les pers de la terre. Et puis dillueqe fust il amene
a une eawe curraunte qest appelle Gaversiche, et illueqes fust il
decole, et ceo fu le xix jour de Juyn le an du regne de cesti
ro[*sic*] quint. Quant le roi avoit oi et entendu coment sire Piers
de Gavestoun estoit mis a la mort par les grantz de la terre, il
estoit durement coroucee et irre, et pensa privement touz jours
en son quoer de sei venger de ceuz qi feurent assentaunz a sa
mort quant il verroit temps. *En meismes cel an frere Vital del*
ordre des menours fu fet cardinal, et meismes lan le jour de seint
Brice sire Edward ficz au cesti roi Edward fu nee a Wyndesore,
et une cardinal qavoit a noum Arnold li leva du founs le jour de
Esmon lercevesqe.

   Lan Mille CCCXIII Robert de Wynchelse ercevesqe de Caunterburi
murust et est enterre a Caunterbury le ix kalend de Juyn lendemain
del Ascencion, et fu mis en son lieu par le pape et a la priere de cesti
roi Edward, sire Waltier Reynaud qi devant fut evesqe de Wyrcestre.
Meisme cel an en la fest de Pentecoust, Lowiz ficz le roi Philippe
de Fraunce fu coroune roi de Naverne, le quel regioun li
descendist de droit et heretablement par sa mere Johanne roigne
de Fraunce, qe fust heire del region de Naverne, as queux
noeces y cesti roi ove Isabelle sa compaigne et plusours graunz
de cest terre feurent. Et cesti roi Edward despendist illuqes a
ceo qe fu dist plus de lx mille livres. Meisme cel an murust
lemperour de Rome en les parties de Tuscy.

   Lan Mille CCCXIIII et de cesti roi vii, le roi assembla grant
houst et grant poer a la Pentecouste, il se mist vers Escoz pur
destuire Robert le Bruys et les altres sez enemis. Et quant il
estoit illueqe venuz le jour de seint Johan le Babtistre

(fo. 250)

St John ante Portam Latinam [6 May], the papal council at Vienne was brought to an end; in this council the order of Templars was abolished. In the same year the lords of the land cleverly and with cunning pursued the said sir Piers Gaveston so that about the time of the feast of St Botolph [17 June] the said sir Piers came to Deddington near to Oxford, and the earl of Warwick seized him by force and took him to the castle of Elmley and from there to Warwick where he was judged by the peers of the land. And then from there he was taken to a stream which is called Gaversiche and there he was beheaded; and this was on 19 June in the fifth year of this king's reign [1312]. When the king heard and understood how sir Piers Gaveston had been put to death by the lords of the country he was greatly angered and annoyed and he secretly contemplated in his heart all the time how to revenge himself when he should see the opportunity on those who had assented to his death. In the same year brother Vitale of the order of friars minor was made a cardinal, and the same year on the day of the feast of St Brice [13 November], sir Edward, the son of this king Edward, was born at Windsor, and a cardinal named Arnold baptised him on the feast of Edmund, the archbishop [16 November].

In 1313 Robert Winchelsey, the archbishop of Canterbury, died and was buried at Canterbury on the ninth day before the kalends of June [24 May], the day after the Ascension,[4] and sir Walter Reynolds who had previously been bishop of Worcester was put in his place by the pope and at the request of this king Edward. In the same year at the feast of Pentecost [3 June], Louis, the son of king Philip of France, was crowned king of Navarre; this region came to him by right and by way of inheritance through his mother Joan, the queen of France, who was the heiress of Navarre; this king [Edward] with Isabella, his consort, and many lords of this land had been present at his celebrations. And this king Edward spent there, according to rumour, more than sixty thousand pounds. In the same year the emperor of Rome died in Tuscany.

In 1314 and the seventh year of this king, the king assembled a large army and great forces at Pentecost and set off for Scotland to destroy Robert Bruce and others of his enemies. And when he had arrived there, on the day of St John the Baptist [24 June],

[4] 25 May: this is an error as Ascension day itself was 24 May in 1313.

(fo. 250v)

Robert le Bruys li vint encontre od grant poer a Stryvely et li dona fort bataille, en qel bataille le roi fust descomfist, et en cele descomfetour furent occis sire Gilbert de Clare counte de Gloucestre, sire Robert de Clifford, sire Payn Tybtot, sire William Maresschal, sire Miles de Stapeltoun, sire William de Vescy, sire Gyles de Argentein, sire William Dayncourt, sire Esmon de Mauley, et multz des altres. Et plusours nobles et puissantz come monsire Humfrey de Bohun counte de Herford et altres graunz Dengleterre furent pris et emprisonez par les Escoz a Bodeville, et puis furent delivres pur greve ransoun. Et le counte de Penbrok, sire Hugh le Dispenser, sire de Beaumont, sire Johan de Cromwell et altres se mistrent a la feute tanqe a Donbarre, et la se mistrent il en eawe od graunt poer et vindrent a Berewyk qe adonqe estoit en gard des Engleis. En cel temps fu pris aval la croice del clocher de seint Pool de Loundres, en la quele furent multz des reliqes trouvez, et ele fust reparaille et mis sus od ceux reliqes et altres le jour (eody: *deleted in red*) de seint Fraunceis apres la seint Michel, et a cel jour chauntauntz divers chanounes et vikers de la dit eglise,[5] plus haut qe la croice nest de xl pees, et grant lumere de torches et altres diverses melodis a donqes estoit illueqes, pur la solempnite des reliqes qen la croice adonqe furent mis. Meisme cel an murust Philippe roi de Fraunce la veille de seint Andreu.

Lan Mille CCCXV meistre Robert[6] de Mortyvaux, dean de Nichole, fust eslu evesqe de Salesbury en tour la Pentecoust. Meisme cel an fu grant habundance deawe en Engleterre quant les murs de les freres menors Deverwyk trebucha par cel eawe entour le feste de seint Margarete. Denapres meisme cel an le roi Edward et altres de son prive conseille sanz assent des graunz de la terre ordinerent assises et certein pris des vitails folement, qi ne poeit en nul manere estre tenu ne meintenu, cest assavoir le meillour boef peu de greyn al plus haut pur xxiiij sous, le meillour boef gras

---

[5] CUL MS Mm.1.33, fo. 59 adds *sur estaches.*
[6] *Recte* Roger.

(fo. 250v)

Robert Bruce met him with a great force at Stirling and engaged him strongly in battle; in this battle the king was defeated, and in this reverse sir Gilbert de Clare, earl of Gloucester, sir Robert Clifford, sir Payn Tiptoft, sir William Marshal, sir Miles Stapleton, sir William Vescy, sir Giles d'Argentein, sir William Dayncourt, sir Edmund Mauley and many others were killed. And many noble and powerful men such as sir Humphrey Bohun, earl of Hereford, and other English lords were taken and imprisoned by the Scots at Bothwell, and were subsequently freed for a heavy ransom. And the earl of Pembroke, sir Hugh Despenser, sir [Henry] Beaumont, sir John Cromwell and others fled as far as Dunbar, and there put to sea in great numbers and came to Berwick which was then garrisoned by the English. At this time the cross was taken down from the steeple at St Paul's in London. In it were many relics; and it was repaired and put back up with these relics and others on St Francis's day after Michaelmas [4 October], and on that day there was chanting by various canons and vicars of the said church (on staging) forty feet higher than the cross; and at that time there was a great light from torches and various other music there, because of the great importance of the relics that were placed in the cross. In this year on St Andrew's eve [29 November] Philip king of France died.

In 1315 master [Roger] Martival, the dean of Lincoln, was elected bishop of Salisbury about the time of Pentecost [11 May]. In the same year there were great floods in England so that the walls of the Greyfriars at York collapsed because of this water about the feast of St Margaret [20 July]. Subsequently in the same year king Edward and others of his privy council, without the assent of the lords of the land, foolishly decreed assises and certain prices of provisions which could in no way be enforced and upheld: that is to say, in London, the best ox fed on grain at most for 24 shillings, the best fat ox

(fo. 251)

nient peu de greyn por xvj sous, la meilloure vache gras pur xij sous, une pork de deux annz pur xxx deners, une motoun toundu et gras pur xiiij deners, une owe gras pur iij deners, une chapon gras pur ij deners obole, une geline pur ij deners, trois columbes pur j dener, xx oefs pur j dener en Loundres. (La: *interlined*) quele prive ordinance fu crie en Loundres la veille des paumes, et fist grant mal, qar en poi de temps apres lem ne poeit a peine rien de tiele chose trouver. Par quei multz des bochers et poleters de Loundres feurent emprisonez et empoveritz, et le commun poeple avoit grant defaute de tiele chose, et mult se plenount, par qei altrefoitz fust purveu par comandement le roi et son dit feble conseil, qi de tieles purveaunces avoit issi esvoegli la gent, qom achateroit et vendroit auxi bon marche come il poeit, qar cele porveaunce ne fust onqes ordene par les ordenies ne par les sages de la terre, mes par le roi et son prive conseil pur esvoegler le commun poeple come de sus est dist. Tost apres cel temps faillerent les bledz par tute Engleterre, et ceo fu pur la graunt eawe qi cheist continuelment de la Pentecoust tanqe a la Pasqe prochein ensiwant, dount il avoit grante morine des gentz, et dura la graunt chierte des bledz continuelement par trois annz, issint qen une sesoune de cele chierte len vendist le quartre de forment malement nette et eschargement mesuree pur xl sous, et deux petites oynons en chepe pur une dener.

Lan Mille CCCXVI Lowis roi de Fraunce ficz levantdit Philippe (murust: *interlined*) devant la feste de Pentecoust. *Mesmes cel an sire Johan de Hothum fust eslu evesqe Dely, et sire Johan de Sandal fu fet evesqe de Wyncestre, et sire William de Meltoun fust eslu ercevesqe Deverwyk, le quel sire William retorna de la court entour la feste de Touz Seintz.*

Lan Mille CCCXVII deux cardinals cestasavoir sire Gauceline et sire Lucas de Fisco alerent vers Duresme pur la consecracion sire Lowys de Beaumont en leveschee de Duresme, et enchiminant les encontrerent sire Gilbert de Middletoun et altres meffesours, et les robberent et despoillerent, le quel sire Gilbert fu pris et amene a Loundres, et illueqes entour la feste de la Purificacion de Nostre Dame fut illueqe

(fo. 251)

not fed on grain for 16 shillings, the best fat cow for 12 shillings, a two year old pig for 30 pence, a shorn and fat sheep for 14 pence, a fat goose for three pence, a fat capon for twopence halfpenny, a hen for twopence, three doves for one penny, 20 eggs for one penny. This privy ordinance was proclaimed in London on the eve of Palm Sunday [15 March] and did much harm; for within a short time afterwards people could hardly find any such things. Because of it many of the butchers and poulterers of London were imprisoned and impoverished and the common people experienced a great shortage of such commodities and complained a great deal. In response to this it was again decreed by order of the king and his weak council, who by such regulations had so misled the people, that they should buy and sell as cheaply as they could; for this regulation was never made by the Ordainers nor by the wise men of the land, but by the king and in his privy council to mislead the common people as is mentioned above. Soon after this time the crops failed throughout the whole of England and this was because of the heavy rain which fell continually from Pentecost through to the next Easter following. On account of this there was great loss of life among the people and the high price of wheat lasted continuously for three years, so that in one season of this price inflation a quarter of wheat badly cleaned and meanly weighed was sold for 40 shillings, and two small onions in Cheapside for one penny.

In 1316 Louis, king of France, the son of the aforesaid Philip, died before the feast of Pentecost [30 May]. In the same year sir John Hotham was elected bishop of Ely, sir John Sandale was made bishop of Winchester, and sir William Melton was elected archbishop of York; this sir William returned from the papal court about the feast of All Saints [1 November].[7]

In 1317 two cardinals, namely sir Gauceline and sir Lucas dei Fieschi, travelled towards Durham for the consecration of sir Lewis de Beaumont in the bishopric of Durham, and on the journey sir Gilbert Middleton and other evil-doers met them and robbed and plundered them. The said sir Gilbert was captured and taken to London and there, about the feast of the Purification of Our Lady [2 February, 1318], he was

---

[7] This was in 1317: Melton spent almost two years at the papal court in Avignon, being elected in January 1316 and consecrated in September 1317.

(fo. 251v)

traine, pendu, decole et desmembre. Meismes cel an en la feste
de seint Valentyn murust la roigne Margarete et gist enterre a
les freres menors de Loundres, et en cel an dame Aleyse la fille
le counte de Nichole et (et: *repeated*) la femme sire Thomas
counte de Lancastre departist del poer son seignur, et sire Johan
counte de Garenne la resceut en sa gard. Meismes cel an avint
issi tost apres le roi tint parlement a Everwyk et la les pers de la
terre par lour commun assent (elurent: *interlined*) sire Hugh le
Despenser le ficz chef chambreleyn le roi, a demorer ove li en
office de chambreleyn solonc son port, le quel sire Hugh fu
plein de malveiste et felonie, et auxint fust il avers et coveitous
tant come il estoit en son office, et si estoit il orguillous et
hautein et compassant de felonye, qe nul homme plus, quar
nul homme purra aprocher au roi sanz la volunte le dist sire
Hugh, et ceo pur grandement doner de soen. Et si nul desiroit
parler ove le roi il noseroit pas en nul manere fors soulement
en la presence de meismes celi sire Hugh. Cesti sire Hugh
acrocha a lui roial poer, si qe le roi ne voleit rien faire countre
sa volunte. Lez comandementz de dit sire Hugh par tut et en
toute places furent faitz et esploitez a sa volunte, et chescune
homme se dota de li, et lui haierent durement de quoer tut
noseient ils rien parler. Il amenusa les services et les despenses
le roi en son hostel. Il acrocha a lui graunt tresor parmy le
roialme, dount ceo fu merveille a dire et countere. Le roi en
quanqe il savoit et poeit lamoit cherement sour touz altres,
issint qil navoit en la terre grant seignur qe oseit faire ou dire
encountre sa volunte des choses qil vodra aver fait.

Lan Mille CCCXVIII le roi tint parlement a Northamtoun
ove touz les grauntz seignurs de la terre. Les pers de la terre
feurent adonqe aperceu en multz des maners de la felonie,
malveiste et coveitise del dit sire Hugh, et del damage qil fist al
roialme par abbettement de sire Hugh le Despenser son pere,
et li voleient aver remue de son office et mettre autre en son
lieu. Meis le roi ne voleit pas suffrir, meis lui tint prede lui et li
maintenist en tuttes choses a sa volunte et od tut son poer,
issint qe les peres de la terre de cel bosoigne

(fo. 251v)

drawn, hanged, beheaded, and quartered. The same year on St Valentine's day [14 February], queen Margaret died and lies buried in the Greyfriars at London; and the same year lady Alice, the daughter of the earl of Lincoln and the wife of sir Thomas earl of Lancaster, left the control of her lord, and sir John, earl Warenne, took her into his protection. The same year, soon after, it so happened that the king held parliament at York and there the peers of the land by their common assent chose sir Hugh Despenser the son, chief chamberlain of the king to stay with him in the office of chamberlain at the king's pleasure. This sir Hugh was full of evil and wrongdoing, and he was also greedy and covetous while he was in office. He was also proud and haughty, more inclined to wrongdoing than any other man, so that no one was able to approach the king without the consent of the said sir Hugh and even then only through making large gifts. And if anyone wished to speak with the king he would not dare do this in any way except only in the said sir Hugh's presence. This sir Hugh appropriated to himself royal power so that the king was not willing to do anything contrary to his wishes. The said sir Hugh's instructions were carried out and put into effect everywhere and in all places according to his will, and everyone feared him and hated him from the bottom of their hearts. Nevertheless they did not dare say anything. He reduced the household services and expenses of the king. He accumulated great wealth for himself throughout the realm, which was marvellous to tell and· relate. The king loved him dearly with all his heart and mind, above all others, so that there was not in the land any great lord who, against sir Hugh's will, dared to do or say the things he would have liked to have done.

In 1318 the king held parliament at Northampton with all the great lords of the land. The peers of the land saw at that time in many ways the wrongdoing, evil, and covetousness of the said sir Hugh, and the damage which he did to the kingdom with the aid of sir Hugh his father, and they wished to have him removed from his office and to put another in his place, but the king would not allow it. On the contrary he kept him close to himself and he supported him in all things, according to his own wishes, and with all his power, so that the peers of the land could not do anything at this stage about this situation.

(fo. 252)

ne poient adonqe rien faire. Avint issi qe tant come le roi tint son parlement, une Johan Poydras par noum qi fu fiz dun tanour de la cite Dexcestre vint a Oxenfod et entra la sale le roi a [sic] les freres cordeilles[8] come le deable li mist en quoer, et auxint il amena ove lui petite charette et une chate, et dist as touz qil fu droit heir Dengleterre, et qil dust estre roi par resoun et noun pas le roi Edward. La gent li demaunderent coment ceo poeit estre, et il lour dist coment et en quel manere qe pur moi ne sera mis en escripte ne reherce. La gent li comanderent de teiser de tieles paroles qe toucherent si haut chose, et il respondist qil ne voleit pur rien qe purroit avenire, par quei il fust amene a Northamtoun au parlement le roi et la fust il examine de sa chalenge, et tut dis il maintenist sa querele devant tuttes gentz, et dist apertement et baudement qil dust estre roi de droit et de reisoun. Ceux qe feurent ditz son pere et sa mere a Excestre feurent mandez au roi el dit parlement, et par le conseil le roi feurent il examinez et sermenteez sur ceste chose, de dire la verite sil estoit lour ficz ou noun, et eux pur poer de la mort noserent altrement dire meis qe il fust lour ficz entre eux engendrez. Et le roi ne li voleit pas aver mis a la mort, mes comanda qome li donast un mascu, en engleis babel, et qil alast come fol. Meis ascuns graunz qe la feurent ne voleient ceo suffrire mes qil fust mis a la mort, issint qil fust traine et pendu a Northamtoun la veille de seint Jak, par quei homme parla mult dun et de ele.

Lan Mille CCCXIX en tour la feste de la Marie Magdaleyne, monsire Thomas counte de Lancastre ove altres grantz de la terre assemblerent grant ost et grant poer pur passer en Escoz, a destruire Robert le Bruys par comaundement le pape pur sa desoltisance qil avoit enfrenit la suffrance de guerre, la quel lavandit pape avoit establi entre le roi Dengleterre et lui, issint qils passerent avant od lor ost par mer et par terre vers la dit regioun Descoce. Meis quant le roi et touz les grauntz de la terre feurent venuz a Noef Chastel sur Tyne, et illueques il tindrent une conseil, et ordeinerent et counseillerent entre eux, coment ils poient conquere la ville de Berewyk qe adonqe estoit bien garni des gentz et de vitalles, et issint ordeinerent entre eux, qe le roi meismes

---

[8] *Recte* carmes: see Bodleian Library MS Lyell 17, fo. 113v.

(fo. 252)

It so happened that, when the king held his parliament, a certain man, John Poydras by name, who was a tanner's son from the city of Exeter, came to Oxford and entered the king's hall and that of the [Carmelites], as the devil put it into his heart, and he also brought with him a little carriage and a cat and told everyone that he was the true heir of England and that by right he ought to be king and not Edward. People asked him how this could be and he told them how and in what way; so far as I am concerned, this will not be put in my text or repeated. He was told to cease talk of this kind which touched such great matters and he replied that he would not do so on any account, whatever might happen. Because of this he was taken to Northampton to the king's parliament and there he was examined about his claim, and before everyone he maintained his contention in everything he said and stated openly and confidently that he ought to be king by right and reason. Those who were said to be his father and mother at Exeter were summoned to the king at the said parliament and they were examined and put on oath by the king's council to tell the truth about this matter, whether he was their son or not. And for fear of death, they did not dare to say otherwise than that he was their son begotten between them. The king did not wish to have him put to death but ordered that he be given a club, in English 'a bauble', and that he go around as a fool, but certain lords who were there did not wish to accept this but wanted him to be put to death, with the result that he was drawn and hanged at Northampton on the eve of St James [24 July], concerning which there was much talk one way and another.

In 1319 about the feast of Mary Magdalene [22 July], sir Thomas earl of Lancaster with other lords of the land assembled a great army and great force to go to Scotland, to destroy Robert Bruce at the pope's order for the devastation by which he had infringed the truce which the aforesaid pope had established between the king of England and him. The result was that they advanced with their army by sea and by land towards Scotland. When the king and all the lords of the land had arrived at Newcastle-upon-Tyne, they held a council there and planned and discussed among themselves how they could conquer the town of Berwick which was then well provisioned with men and supplies. So they planned among themselves that the king himself

(fo. 252v)

et touz les graunz de la terre devoient primes enseger la dist
ville de Berewyk et la gayner par force avant qils alassent avant
en la terre, et ceo fu par enchesoun qe le roi et les grantz voleient
aver bon refut dedeinz la dite ville si cas de peril lour avensist
en la dite terre Descoz, et tantost comaunderent lor purveiors
od grant numbre de gentz darmes passer avant a la dite ville, et
hastivement ficher lour pavillouns et herbergers, et puis faire
bone purveaunce des vitailles et dautres necessaries qe a eux
appendoient pur guerre, et issint le firent. Tost apres le roi et
touz les graunz de la terre se remuerent de la dite ville del Noef
Chastes mult efforcement od lor poer bien bataillez taunqe ils
vindrent dencost la dite ville de Berewyk od trompes clamantz,
et fesoient cele nuyt grant joie et solaz melodie en despit de les
Escoz lor enemis qi feurent dedeinz la dite ville. Meis les Escoz
escrierent noz gentz vilement et horriblement et monterent les
murs de la ville et la defenderent noblement en countre les
Engleis. Et fet assaver qe le jour de lassumpcion de Nostre
Dame qe fu le xviij kalend daugst[9] le roi et les graunz de la terre
et lour gentz donerent fort assaut a la dit ville, mes riens ne
poient espleitre. Le roi fist mandre les engins de Northamtoun
et de Bamburgh, et les fist redescer countre les murs de la dite
ville de Berewyk, et fesoient multz des maux a ceux qi feurent
dedeinz la dite ville. Et ceux qi feurent depar leawe avoient
eniointz lor niefs a les murs de la dit ville, (et: *interlined*)
donerent mult plus fort assaut qe devant navoient, et
combatirent od la navie le roi de la part leawe mult egrement.
Meis les Engleis se defendirent si noblement encountre les
Escoz lour enemis quex navoient encountre eux foisoun ne
dure. Et les Engleis feurent enpoint a cele heure daver conquis
legerment la ville sanz pluis assaut faire si ascuns grantz de la
terre ne eussent este. En cele temps tant come la sege de
Berewyk se dura vindrent en Engleterre pred le paiis de
Cardoille Thomas Randolf counte de Mouref et James Dougleis
ove xx mille Descoz bien combatantz,

---

[9] *Recte* Septembre.

(fo. 252v)

and all the lords of the land should first besiege the said town of Berwick and gain control of it by force before proceeding further into the country. And this was because the king and the lords wished to have a good refuge within the said town in case danger should come upon them in the said land of Scotland. And they immediately ordered their purveyors with a great number of men at arms to go ahead to the said town and quickly erect their tents and lodgings and then to make good provision for foodstuffs and other necessities which were essential for them to make war, and so they did. Soon after the king and all the lords of the land left the said town of Newcastle, increased in strength, with their force well arrayed, until they came up to the said town of Berwick with trumpets blowing and spent the night in great joy and pleasure [and] music in contempt of their Scottish enemies who were inside the said town. But the Scots shouted out at our people foully and hideously and climbed onto the walls of the town and defended it honourably against the English. And be it known that on the day of the Assumption of Our Lady [15 August], which was the eighteenth day before the kalends of [September] the king and the lords of the land and their followers launched a great attack on the said town but could accomplish nothing. The king had the siege engines sent up from Northampton and Bamburgh and had them drawn up against the walls of the said town of Berwick and caused much injury to those who were inside the town. And those who were on the seaward side had moored their ships to the walls of the said town and they delivered a much more vigorous assault than they had previously done, and they [the Scots] fought most bitterly with the king's fleet on the seaward side. The English defended themselves so honourably against their Scottish enemies that these had neither the resources nor stamina to hold their ground. And the English were at this time on the point of having conquered the town easily without making a further attack, if certain of the lords of the land had not been there. At this time while the siege of Berwick was proceeding there came to England, in the vicinity of Carlisle, Thomas Randolph, earl of Moray, and James Douglas with twenty thousand well armed Scots,

(fo. 253)

et les jours les embosoignerent et demorerent en boys et en marreis longteyn des villes, issint qe gentz du paiis ne poeient aver conussance de eux, et nutantre chivauchierent od lor ost, tanqe ils vindrent au pount de Burgh et Mitoun sur Swale qe nest qe xii lues hors Deverwyk, et voleint aver passe outre a la cite Deverwyk et aver conquis la ville od force. Meis tost vindrent novels a sire William de Meltoun ercevesqe de la citee et a sire Johan de Hotham qi adonqe estoit chauneller [sic] le roi, et tantost ils assemblerent tot le poer qils poeient cuiller et procurer a eux. *Et une Nichol Flemmynge qi adonqe estoit maire de la dit citee, noblee homme et vaillaint, ove plusors de la cite sen alerent efforcement od tut lor poer devers Mitoun pur countre estere la malice des Escoz lour enemis. Et quant eux feurent venuz a Mitoun od le aide du paiis, ils se drescerent pur donerent bataille a les Escoz lor enemis. Mais les Escoce, qi feurent gentz de bone arraie et bien apparaillez a (a: repeated) la guerre, avoient grant despit des Engleis, et maintenant comencerent a tromper et sanz plus delai se mistrent a les Engleis pur combatre, meis les Engleis furent tost occis et descomfitz, et plusors neiez en leawe de Swale, dount li doels estoit, et le dite Nichol Flemenge illueques fu destrenche et desmembre tut en peces, et lercevesqe sire William de Meltoun, et sire Johan de Hothum chaunceller sen feuirent tant come ils poient a la cite Deverwyk, et firent fermere les portz et la se tindrent.* Meis sire William de Ayremyn, noble clerk et vaillant, fu pris illueqe et mene en Escoce et mis en garde, et puis fu delivres par greve raunson. Quant le roi Edward avoit oi et entendu coment les Escoz avoient ensi destruit le gentz de sa terre come devant est dit, maintenant il remua sa sege et ala a Loundres mult dolent. *Meismes cel an le jour de Touz Seintz morust sire Johan de Sandal evesqe de Wyncestre. Et en la feste de la Epiphanie prochein siwant sire (Johan: interlined) de Dalderby feu fet evesqe de Nichole.[10] Et apres li fust eslu meistre Antoyn de Bek chaunceller de Nichole en la feste de seint Agnes*

---

[10] The text is in error: Dalderby died this year, as the rest of the sentence makes clear.

(fo. 253)

and during the day they occupied and stayed in woods and marshes far from the towns, so that the people of the area should have no knowledge of them, and at night they rode with their army until they reached Boroughbridge and Myton-on-Swale which was only twelve leagues from York. They wished to go on to the city of York and to take the city by force, but soon news reached sir William Melton archbishop of the city, and sir John Hotham, who was then the king's chancellor, and immediately they assembled all the force that they could gather and raise for themselves. And a certain Nicholas Fleming who was then the mayor of the said city, a noble and valiant man, went with many others from the city in strength with all their force towards Myton to oppose the malice of their Scottish enemies. And when they had come to Myton, with the support of the local people, they formed up to give battle to their Scottish enemies. But the Scots, who were well marshalled and well equipped for war, had great scorn for the English and now began to sound their trumpets and without further delay began to fight the English and soon the English were killed and defeated; many were drowned in the River Swale, over which there was sorrow, and the said Nicholas Fleming was there cut down and dismembered. The archbishop, sir William Melton, and sir John Hotham, the chancellor, fled as best they could to the city of York and closed the gates and remained there. But sir William Ayremynne, a noble and valiant clerk, was captured there and taken to Scotland, imprisoned, and was subsequently freed for a heavy ransom.[11] When king Edward had heard and understood how the Scots had thus destroyed the people of his land as described above he abandoned the siege and went to London grief-stricken. The same year on All Saints day [1 November], sir John Sandale the bishop of Winchester died, and on the feast of the Epiphany [6 January] next following sir John Dalderby, bishop of Lincoln, [died], and after him, on the second feast day of St Agnes [28 January], master Anthony Bek chancellor of Lincoln was elected;

---

[11] This is a fuller account of the encounter at Myton-on-Swale than that found in any other text of the short continuation of the *Brut*.

(fo. 253v)

la secunde, meis il ne fust pas resceu par lercevesqe de Caunterbury, et pur ceo il alast a la coute [sic] de Rome, et demura ove le pape.

Lan Mille CCCXX la pape dona a sire Henry de Burghassh leveschee de Nichole et fust entronize al Noel ensiwant.

Lan Mille CCCXXI morust sire Walter de Langetoun evesqe de Cestre, et fu mis en son lieu sire Roger de Northburgh a la priere de cesti roi Edward. Meismes cel an morust Philippe roi (de Fraunce et est: *interlined*) enterre a seint Denys, mes son quoer est enterre a les frere minors de Parys, ou son primer ficz est enterre, et apres cesti roi Philippe Caroille son frere fu fet roi de Fraunce.

Lan Mille CCCXXII a la goule daugst le roi tint parlement a Westminstre, au queu parlement vindrent le counte de Hereford, les Mortumers, le Moubray, le Clifford, et plusours autres grantz de la terre od grant poer, et vindrent a Loundres touz armez noun pas en despit du roi, meis pur ouster sez malveis conseillers come sire Hugh le Despenser le piere, et le ficz. Et a cel parlement les avantditz counte de Hereford, Mortumers, et les autres susditz monstrerent au roi lour grevances encountre les deux Despensers, par qei en la veille del Assumpcion de Notre Dame en la presence du roi, countes, barons et la commune Dengleterre aux feurent exillez a Westminstre hors du roialme Dengleterre come traitres, sur (paine: *interlined*) decapitacion, sils james revenissent en le poer et la seignurie le roi. Et adonqes sire Hugh le Despenser le piere se mist hastivement outre meer, et dona a son ficz sa malison, qar pur son malveis port il avoit cel aventure encorue. Et le roi maintenist le Despenser le ficz el roialme par mie laide de les cink portz par meer, issint qe cheli Hugh le Despenser le ficz, ove le poer a li atreit, robba par mier dromontz qi feurent envenantz vers Engleterre ove grant noumbre davoire, et autres nefs en esclaundre du roi et de touz ceux du roi, la quele robberie fist grant mal al roialme et grante parlaunce y fust par tut le roialme. Et le pape escomengea touz y ceux qi feissent cele robberie ou qi fuissent a ceo assentant. En cel temps

(fo. 253v)

but he was not accepted by the archbishop of Canterbury and because of this he went off to the court of Rome and remained with the pope.

In 1320 the pope gave the bishopric of Lincoln to sir Henry Burghersh and he was enthroned the following Christmas.

In 1321 sir Walter Langton, bishop of Chester, died, and sir Roger Northburgh was put in his place at the request of this king Edward. In the same year Philip, king of France, died and was buried at St Denis, but his heart was buried at the Franciscan friary of Paris where his first son was buried, and after this king Philip, Charles his brother was made king of France.

In [1321] on 1 August the king held parliament at Westminster, to which parliament the earl of Hereford, the Mortimers, Mowbray, and Clifford and many other lords of the land came with great forces; and they came to London completely armed, not in contempt of the king, but to get rid of his evil counsellors such as sir Hugh Despenser, both the father and the son. At this parliament the above mentioned earl of Hereford, the Mortimers, and the others above mentioned made known to the king their grievances against the two Despensers, because of which on the eve of the Assumption of Our Lady [14 August], at Westminster, in the presence of the king, earls, barons, and the community of England, they were exiled from the realm of England as traitors, on pain of beheading if they ever returned into the power and lordship of the king. Then sir Hugh Despenser the father quickly took himself overseas and cursed his son because thanks to his (the son's) evil behaviour he had incurred this misadventure. The king kept Despenser the son in the realm, at sea, with the help of the Cinque Ports, so that this Hugh Despenser the son, with the force gathered by him, robbed at sea dromonds,[12] which were coming to England with a great many goods, and other ships, to the great dishonour of the king and all the king's people. This piracy did great harm to the realm; there was great talk of it through the whole realm, and the pope excommunicated all those who committed this piracy or who were party to it. At this time

---

[12] These were large sailing ships brought from the Mediterranean by Italian merchants, and thus very rich prizes.

la grossure del coer le roi surmonta durement de vengeaunce
faire sour la partie qe lui contraria, ne pur quant il les avoit fet
chartres de pees des totes maneres des felonies, robberies,
arsours, et chivauchees, et totes autres matieres des trespas qe
eux avoient fait en son roialme ou en sa seignurie sur les terres
et chastels de les ditz sire Hugh (et sire Hugh: *deleted in red*),
mes totes celes chartres ne valoient pas, qar il meismes (par
autres mauveis conseille qil avoit, vient encountre)[13] les chartres
qil avoit grante, si qe la corde et la pees entre le roi et sez barons
furent tut outrement defait pur nul tenu. Tost apres a la feste
de seint Michel le roi assembla (grant et: *deleted in red*) grant
poer pur assegere le chastel de (les: *deleted in red*) Ledes, qe fust
a une sire Berthelmeu de Badelesmere, qestoit grant seignur et
le seneschal le roi. Meis il fust tenu homme de mal affaire. En
cel temps vindrent le counte de Herford, les Mortumers, le
Moubray, et autres grantz du roialme ove lour poer a
Kyngestoun sur la ryvere de Thamise, pur aver alee outre a
Ledes a remuer la sege sils poeient, mes le bone counte de
Lancastre lour manda par sez lettres qe ceo ne duissent (ils:
deleted in red) ils faire, par ount une sire Walter Reynaud
ercevesqe de Caunterbury vint a Kyngestoun oue les barons
furent, et illuqe les premist loialment et en bone foi, qe si eux
se voleient retrere de lour pursiwete, qil ferroit bone acord
entre (entre: *repeated*) le roi et eux. Et le gentil counte de
Lancastre manda amiablement au roi par sez lettres, qil cessat
de la persecucion qil comenca affaire sur sez lieges gentz a
reson. Et le roi tint en despit quantqe le gentil counte et autres
grantz li avorent mande, mes (toutz: *interlined*) jours pensa de
sei venger de eux, issint qe le roi entra le chastel de Ledes le
veille de Touz Seintz, et sire Berthelmeu de Burghhasse, et la
dame de Badlesmere, et altres grantz qi furent el chastel furent
mandez a la Tour de Loundres. Et xij autres qi furent el dit
chastel furent illueqes traignez et penduz, meis une Thomas
Colepepre de Kent fust maunde a Wynchelse, et illueqes fust il
traine et pendu, a quele ale al dist chastel de Ledes ceux de
Loundres manderent au roi cink

(fo. 254)

the king's heart was bursting with desire for vengeance on the party which was opposing him, although he had granted them charters of peace for all manner of felonies, robberies, arsons, and raids, and all other matters of offence which they had committed in his realm or in his lordship against the lands and castles of the said [two] sir Hughs, but all these charters were worthless for he (himself, through other evil advice which he took, went against) the same charters which he had granted, so that the accord and peace between the king and his barons were entirely undermined [and] ignored. Soon after, at Michaelmas [29 September], the king assembled a great force to besiege Leeds Castle, which belonged to sir Bartholomew Badlesmere, who was a great lord and the king's steward, but he was considered as a man of evil intent. At this time the earl of Hereford, the Mortimers, Mowbray, and other lords of the realm came with their forces to Kingston on the river Thames, intending to have gone on further to Leeds to raise the siege if they could, but the good earl of Lancaster told them by his letters that they should not do this; whereby a certain sir Walter Reynolds, archbishop of Canterbury, came to Kingston where the barons were and there he promised them loyally and in good faith that if they would retire from their action he would make good accord between the king and them. And the noble earl of Lancaster told the king in a friendly way, by his letters, that in justice he should stop persecuting his liege people. And the king held in contempt what the gentle earl and other lords had told him, but every day thought of revenging himself on them. Thus the king entered Leeds Castle on the eve of All Saints [31 October], and sir Bartholomew Burghersh and lady Badlesmere and other lords who were in the castle were sent to the Tower of London. And twelve others who were in the said castle were drawn and hanged there, but a certain Thomas Culpepper of Kent was sent to Winchelsea and there he was drawn and hanged. To this expedition to the said Leeds Castle the Londoners sent the king

(fo. 254v)

centz hommes a pee bien armeez. En cel temps le counte de Hereford et les autres barons virent bien qe le roi fust homme sanz mercy, et penserent bien qil les voleit destruire si come il avoit fait autres, et pristrent lour chimin vers le north jesqes a Pountfreit, oue le noble counte de Lancastre adonqe estoit pur avere de lui socours et aide, a meintenire la querele qils avoient comence encountre les deux Despensers et autres enemis de la terre. Et tant come ils demurerent en les parties du north, ils ensegerent le chastel de Tykhulle, meis riens ne poeient illueqes espleiter tant fu le chastel fort et bien defendu. Puis apres ils sen departirent dilluqe et vindrent au dit counte de Lancastre et tindrent ove lui grant conseil, pur saver et ordener coment ils poeient mieltz countre estere la malice le roi et de les deux Despensers avantditz, et assemblerent tout lour poer, et passerent vers le paiis de Wyrcestre, et vindrent a Birtoun pur encontrer illueqes les deux Despensers et autres enemis de la terre, et demurerent longement en cel paiis et fesoient moltz des maux. Quant le roi avoit oi et entendu de la venue le barnage en le paiis de Wircestre, il assembla grant ost et grant poer pur destruere son barnage, et ove li demurerent le counte mareschal, Esmond son frere counte de Kente, sire Johan counte de Garenne, sir Johan counte de Richemund, le counte Darundel, le counte Dathels, et le counte de Pembrok et moltz des autres barons ove grandisme ost et poer, et vindrent al pount de la dit ville de Burtoun ou il trouerent grante multitude des archers et dautres gentz darmes, qi les defendist vigerousement le passage, mes le roi et les soens passerent leawe a une gye qi fu pres de illueqe. Et quant le counte de Lancastre ceo savoit, hastivement ove les soens senfuist dillueqe tantqe a Pontefreid. Et le roi ove le soen ost sen ala a Wircestre pur espier et enquere plusours meffesours en la terre et contreestere la malice de eux, a quele alee ceux de Loundres manderent autrefoiz au roi a Wircestre a la feste de seint Lucie iij^c iiij^{xx} hommes a pee bien armez. En cel

500 well-armed footmen. At this time the earl of Hereford and the other barons saw full well that the king was a man without mercy, and thought indeed that he would destroy them as he had done others, and thus they made their way northwards as far as Pontefract, where the noble earl of Lancaster then was, to have his support and help in maintaining the cause which they had begun against the two Despensers and other enemies of the land. And while they stayed in northern parts they besieged the castle of Tickhill but could achieve nothing there, so strong and well-defended was the castle. Then, afterwards, they left there and came to the said earl of Lancaster and held long discussions with him in order to find out and decide how they might best oppose the evil intentions of the king and the two aforesaid Despensers, and they assembled all their forces and went towards the Worcester area and came to Burton in order to confront there the two Despensers and other enemies of the land, and they stayed a long time in that vicinity and did much damage. When the king had heard and learnt of the arrival of the baronage in the Worcester area he assembled a great army and great force to destroy his baronage and with him were the earl marshal, Edmund, his brother, the earl of Kent, sir John, earl Warenne, sir John, earl of Richmond, the earl of Arundel, the earl of Atholl, the earl of Pembroke and many of the other barons, with a very great army and force. They came to the bridge of the said town of Burton where they found a great multitude of archers and other men-at-arms who vigorously defended the crossing against them, but the king and his men crossed the water at a ford which was nearby. And when the earl of Lancaster realized this, he fled in haste with his men from there to Pontefract. And the king with his forces went to Worcester to seek out and enquire after many evildoers in the land and to put an end to their wickedness. To this expedition at the feast of St Lucy [15 December] the Londoners sent again 380 well-armed footmen to the king at Worcester. At this

(fo. 255)

temps sire Hugh le Despenser le piere, qi fust exile, revint en
Engleterre ove poer qil poeit a ly attrere pur afforcer sa partie
en conseil et en fait. Puis avint issint qe a la feste de la conversion
de seint Poel par compassement des messages,[14] freres et altres,
qui vindrent par entre le roi et les deux Mortumers come faux
brokors, et firent tant par lour engin et compassement, qe les
Mortumers vindrent au roi come en forme de pees et de treter
dacord entre les parties. Et quant auxi furent venuz au roi eux
ne poient mie passer hors de son poer, mes furent arrestutz et
maundes a la Tour de Loundres, et la vindrent ils le samady
apres manger en la veille de seint Valentyn. En cel temps le
tiers jour de Marcz ceux de Loundres manderent au roi vj[xx]
hommes bien armez, qar il noseient autrement faire pur doute
de sa felonie, ne pur quant la volente del commune poeple fust
enclinant a la partie des countes et barouns privement, come ils
oseient dire et monstrer, pur espiers qi feurent par tut espiant
et enquerant ceo qe homme dist et parloit. Meisme cel an le xvj
jour de Marcz qe adonqe fu le mardi prochein apres la feste de
seint Gregoire, fu sire Thomas counte de Lancastre pris au
pount de Burgh par une sire Andreu de Hercclay et autres qui
vindrent illueqe od grant poer, et illueqe de sur la ponte de la
dit ville le noble counte de Hereford fust occis, et sire William
de Sule, sire Roger de Bromsfeld (et sir Rauf de Elpingdon
adonqe tuez et multz des gentz)[15] de la terre pris et emprisonez,
lour terres et lour chateux en la main le roi seisiz, et
plusors autres vaillantz chivalers et esquiers eschaperent mult
cheitivement outre mier, pur doute destre maumene. Le dit
sire Andreu de Herccla amena le dit counte de Lancastre a
Everwyk, et la fust il mis en garde en la haut tour du chastel de
meisme la citee. Meis tost apres le roi li maunda tanqe a
Pountfreit le quel lieu le dit counte amast plus qe nul autre ville
de la terre. Et illuqes le roi fust entre le chastel le dit counte, et
ove li sire Hugh li encontra et li le denga par malicious paroles
et despitouses en my son visage en despit de li. Le quel (sire
Hugh),[16] sire Esmond

---

[14] 'Messagers' in Bodleian Library MS Lyell 17, fo. 114v, and in other texts.
[15] Bodleian Library MS Lyell 17, fo. 114v.
[16] Ibid.

(fo. 255)

time sir Hugh Despenser the father, who had been exiled, returned to England with what force he could attract to himself, to strengthen his side in advice and in deed. Then it so happened, at the feast of the Conversion of St Paul [25 January, 1322], by the conspiracy of messengers, his brothers and others, who came back and forth between the king and the two Mortimers like false brokers, and did so much by their cunning and conspiring, that the Mortimers came to the king as in peace and to treat of accord between the two parties. And when they had thus come to the king they were unable in any way to leave his power, but were arrested and sent to the Tower of London and they arrived there on Saturday after dinner on the eve of St Valentine's day [13 February]. At this time, 3 March, the Londoners sent to the king 120 well-armed men, for they dared not do otherwise for fear of his wickedness; nonetheless the will of the common people was inclining towards the side of the earls and barons, [but] secretly, because they dared [not] say and show this, on account of spies who were seeking out and enquiring everywhere into what was said and spoken. In the same year, on 16 March which was then Tuesday following the feast of St Gregory [Friday, 12 March], sir Thomas, earl of Lancaster, was taken at Boroughbridge by a certain sir Andrew Harclay and others who came there with large forces; and there on the bridge of the said town the noble earl of Hereford was killed, and there also sir William de Sully, sir Roger Bromsfeld (and sir Ralph Elpingdon were killed, and many people) of the land taken and imprisoned, their lands and their castles taken into the king's hand; and many other valiant knights and esquires escaped most wretchedly overseas for fear of being badly dealt with. The said sir Andrew Harclay took the said earl of Lancaster to York and there he was put under guard in the high tower of the castle of the same city, but soon after the king sent him to Pontefract, a place the said earl loved more than any other town in the land. And there the king had entered the said earl's castle and, sir Hugh being with him, met the earl and contemptuously insulted him to his face with malicious and arrogant words. This (sir Hugh), sir Edmund,

(fo. 255v)

counte Darundelle et sire Robert de Marbelthorpe furent faitz
sez justices, par le roi et la par record du roi qe adonqe fust
tenue pur lei, ils lui jugerent estre decole le xx jour de Marcz,
cest assaver le jour de seint Cuthbert, en une lieu le quel le dit
counte ama mult de haunter pur soi deduire, et (ceo fu: *interlined*)
par my cel decapitacion sire Pieres de Gavastoun avant nome
qi le roi milt [*sic*] ama. Allas, quel dolour fust, qar meisme le
jour qe le noble counte fuist issint decole pur son grant loialte
qil avoit de maintenir droiture et la coroune le roi pur commun
profist de toute le roialme, sis grantz seignurs barouns furent
ovesqe li par my Pountfreit traynez et penduz, cest assaver sire
William ficz William, sire Garyn del Isle, Henry de Brandborn,
sire Thomas Mauduyt, sire William Cheyne, sire William
Tuchet et une Johan Page vadlet al dit counte, *et sont enterrez a
les freres prechours de Pountfreit. Et le corps del noble counte de
Lancastre fust livere par commandement le roi a les moignes de meissme
la (la:* repeated*) ville, ou son corps gist enterre en lour eglise prede le
haut auter, et tost apres le quart kalend Daveril notre seignur Jesu
Crist (fist:* interlined*) moltz des miracles pur lamur de lui.* Le roi
par tut le paiis fist enquere ou eux furent qil tint sez enemis, et
furent par droit sez amis. Mes il ne savoit entendre, et pur ceo
il les fist traigner et pendre par la ou ils furent mieltz conuz
et avoient lour seignurie, cestassaver sire Berthelmeu de
Badelesmere qi fu seneschal le roi, et homme devant de mal
affaire, meis qil tint ou les piers de la terre pur son serment
sauver, il fust traigne, pendu et decole a Caunterbirs. Et puis le
corps sanz test autrefoicz pendu prede son neveu sire Barthelmeu
de Assheburnham, le meskerdy devant Pasqes une sire Henry
Tyeis treigne et pendu, a Loundres, le samady de Pasqes Florie
une sire Fraunceis de Aldenham traine et pendu, a Wyndesore,
le meskerdy apres la Pasqes Florie sire Johan de Moubray li
noble juvencel, sire Roger de Clifford, et sire Gocelyn Dayville
trainez et pendux a Everwyk, *et pendirent illueqes par longe temps
on cheines de feer, meis puis par le*

(fo. 255v)

earl of Arundel, and sir Robert Mablethorp were appointed his judges by the king, and there by record of the king, which now was taken for law, they condemned him to be beheaded on 20 March, that is St Cuthbert's day, in a place which the said earl liked greatly to frequent for pleasure. And this was [in retaliation] for the beheading of sir Piers Gaveston named above whom the king greatly loved. Alas! what grief there was! For on the same day that the noble earl was thus beheaded for the great faithfulness he had shown in upholding right and the royal estate of the king for the common profit of all the realm, six great lords, barons, were drawn and hanged with him at Pontefract, that is sir William Fitz William, sir Warin de Lisle, Henry Bradbourn, sir Thomas Mauduit, sir William Cheyny, sir William Tuchet and a certain John Page, valet of the said earl, and they were buried at the Dominican friary of Pontefract. And the body of the noble earl of Lancaster was handed over by the king's order to the monks of the same town where his body lies buried in their church close to the high altar. And soon after, on the fourth day before the kalends of April [29 March], Our Lord Jesus Christ did many miracles for love of him. The king had enquiries made throughout the region as to where those whom he held to be his enemies were; and they were in justice his friends, but he would not listen. And for that he had them drawn and hanged wherever they were best known and held their lordship: Sir Bartholomew Badlesmere, who was the king's steward and formerly a man of ill behaviour, but who held with the peers of the land because of his oath, was drawn and hanged and beheaded at Canterbury. And then the headless body was again hanged near his nephew sir Bartholomew Ashburnham. On the Wednesday before Easter [7 April] a certain sir Henry Tyes was drawn and hanged at London; on the Saturday before Palm Sunday [3 April], a certain sir Francis Aldenham was drawn and hanged at Windsor; on Wednesday after Palm Sunday [7 April], sir John Mowbray the noble youth, sir Roger Clifford, and sir Jocelin Dayville were drawn and hanged at York and hung there a long time in iron chains, but then with the

(fo. 256)

congi le roi furent ils pris aval, et sount enterres en la eglise de les freres prechours Deverwyk. Sire Henry de Mountfort et sire Henry de Wylingtoun traignez et penduz a Bristut. Sire Roger de Elmerigge et plusours autres grantz come esquiers, fraunkleyns (furent pris)[17] et autres des queux ascuns furent delivres par greve raunson, ascuns mortz en prisoun et ascuns utlagez. Apres qe le dite vengeane fust issint felonousement pris et faite, le roi meisme cel an se adrescea ove tout son poer vers les parties Descoz, par qei les bones gentz de Loundres, en la ville de seint Margarete lan de son reigne xvj, manderent au roi al Noef Chastel sour Tyne cent hommes bien armez et apparailles. En cel temps le secunde jour daugst les deux Mortumers furent juggez a Westminstre devant sis justices destre traignez et penduz, pur robberiez et homicides qe le roi les mist sur. Mes nul excucion de cel jugement ne fu fait, et ceo fu pur bref le roi, qe fu maunde a sire Roger de Swynardestoun adonqe conestable de la Tour de Loundres pur targer le dit jugement, issint qe lendemaine apres le roi de sa grace les granta vie et membre destre en perpetuele prisone. En cel temps apres a la goule daugst le roi sen ala od grant ost et ove grant poer en les parties Descoz, et fust entre en la terre bien a lx lieux, et illueqes moltz des gentz morurent pur defaute de viaunde, et le roi illueqes riens nespleita, mes se retourna en Engleterre, et son poeple grandement destruit pur defaute de vitailles. Et quant les Escoz savoint qe le roi sen departist hors del roialme Descoz, ils passerent la mere Descoz et hastivement vindrent en Engleterre robbaunt et destruant la terre, et fesoient moltz des maux.

Lan Mille CCCXXIII[18] a la feste de seint[19] Luk le roi estoit sur Blakhowe more prede labbeie de Byland ove plusours nobles de son roialme, et illuqes vint sir Robert de Bruys ove grant poer des Escoz et enchacea le roi et les soens. Meis illueqes fu pris monsire Johan de Bretaigne counte de Richemu[n]d et amene en Escoce ou il fust mis en sauve gard, et demurast illueqe par longe temps. Meis au darrein il

---

[17] Ibid., fo. 115. Both versions clearly omit a phrase after Elmerigge as he was executed at Gloucester.

[18] *Recte* CCCXXII.

[19] *Margin*: Bylandbank.

(fo. 256)

king's permission they were taken down and are buried in the church of the Dominicans of York. Sir Henry Montfort and sir Henry Willington were drawn and hanged at Bristol. Sir Roger Elmerigge[20] and several others, lords and esquires, some franklins and others (were captured), of whom some were released for a heavy ransom, some died in prison, and some were outlawed. After the said vengeance had been thus cruelly taken and exacted, the king in the same year turned his attention with all his forces to Scotland; for which the good people of London, on the eve of St Margaret, in the sixteenth year of his reign [19 July, 1322], sent 100 well-armed and equipped men to the king at Newcastle-upon-Tyne. At this time, 2 August, the two Mortimers were sentenced at Westminster before six justices to be drawn and hanged for robberies and murders of which the king accused them, but no execution of this sentence took place; and this was by the king's writ, which was sent to sir Roger Swinnerton, then constable of the Tower of London, to delay the said sentence, so that, the following day, the king of his grace granted them life and limb in perpetual imprisonment. At this time, after the beginning of August the king went with a great army and with a great force to Scotland and had travelled into the land a good sixty leagues, and there many of his men died for lack of food and the king achieved nothing there but returned to England, and his men had suffered serious loss for lack of provisions. And when the Scots knew that the king had left the realm of Scotland they crossed the Scottish sea and quickly came into England robbing and destroying the land and doing much damage.

In [1322] at the feast of St Luke [18 October], the king was on Blackhowmoor near Byland Abbey with a number of nobles of his realm and sir Robert Bruce came there with a great force of Scots and drove the king and his men away. But sir John of Brittany, earl of Richmond, was captured there and taken into Scotland where he was put into safe custody and there he stayed for a long time. But at last he

[20] See note 17.

(fo. 256v)

fust delivres pur trois mille livres. Et donqe revint en Engleterre entour la feste de seint Lowiz evesqe et confessor. Et par la ove noz gentz en les parties Descoz rien ne gaignerent pur defaute de grace, meis perdirent lour vies et quant ils avoient, les Escoz a lour venue a cele foiz gaignerent vitailles, tresor, chivals et harnois le roi, et autres biens par my le paiis a grant hounte et perdicion de roi et du roialme, et salvement retournerent en Escoce ov lour prei. Et ceo fu par lassent et la suffrerance de monsire Andreu de Herccla, le quel le roi avoit fait counte de Cardoille, pur ceo qil avoit pris le dit counte de Lancastre et occis le counte de Hereford come avant est dist. En cel temps nostre seignur Jhesu, qi cognust totes droiturs, voleit par sa grace signe faire qe le dite gentil counte de Lancastre murust en droit querele pur lestat du roialme maintenire, et qe le poeple deveroit le mieultz crere et entendre, si fist il plousours miracules pur lamour de li qi veraies sont et trouveez par bons examinementz. Et dautrepart homme poeit bien entendre qe le dite gentil counte murust en droit querele, qar ceux qi furent a sa mort assentantz onqes ne vindrent au bone fine come bien sera dist apres. Et[21] auxint sire Andreu de Herccla avant dit, pur ceo qil avoit fait ascuns conspiracions et conferacions ove les Escoz, de les aver amene en Engleterre a destruire le north paiis, dont par maundement le roi et le dit sire Andreu fu pris come traitre el chastell de Cardoille par monsire Antoyn de (de: *repeated*) Lucy, et la fust il traigne, pendu, et decole, sez boels (ars),[22] et quartrone, et sa teste mande a Loundres le dimanche lendemain de seint Gregoire. Des autres qi furent al dit contrariantz de lour mal fine vous eit dit par ordre.

Lan Mille CCCXXIIII[23] le roi vint a Westminstre en la semeigne de Pasqes, et le roi ne voleit parler ove le maire de Loundres ne ovesqe les bones gentz, ne lour present resceivre fors de par la commune, issint qe a les utanes de Pasqes il fist somondre le dit maire, viscountes, et

---

[21] *Margin*: A. Herclay.
[22] Bodleian Library MS Lyell 17, fo. 115v.
[23] *Recte* CCCXXIII.

(fo. 256v)

was ransomed for 3,000 pounds, and so he returned to England about the feast of St Louis bishop and confessor [?25 August, 1324].[24] And while our people in Scotland gained nothing through lack of divine grace, but lost their lives and what they possessed, the Scots in their invasion at this time gained provisions, treasure, horses and harness belonging to the king, and other goods in the country, to the great shame and loss of the king and the realm, and returned safely to Scotland with their booty. And this happened with the agreement and connivance of sir Andrew Harclay whom the king had made earl of Carlisle, because he had captured the said earl of Lancaster and killed the earl of Hereford as has previously been stated. At this time Our Lord Jesus, who is aware of all righteousness, wished of His divine grace to show that the said noble earl of Lancaster had died in a just cause in order to uphold the estate of the realm; and so that the people should the better have faith and believe, He worked a number of miracles for the love of him, which are genuine, and found to be so by good investigations. And in another way people could well understand that the said noble earl had died in a just cause, for those who assented to his death never came to a good end as will be described below, including sir Andrew Harclay previously mentioned because he had entered into plots and conspiracies with the Scots to bring them to England to destroy the north country. For this the said sir Andrew was arrested as a traitor, by order of the king, at Carlisle castle by sir Anthony Lucy and there he was drawn and hanged and beheaded, his bowels (burnt), and quartered, and his head sent to London on Sunday, the day after St Gregory's day [13 March]. The bad end of the others who were with the said contrariants will be told to you in due course.

In [1323] the king came to Westminster in Easter week [c. 27 March], and the king was not willing to speak with the mayor of London nor with the good people [of the city], nor to receive their gift except on behalf of the commune. The result was that at the octave of Easter [3 April] he had the said mayor, sheriffs, and

[24] See above p. 44.

(fo. 257)

adermains [*sic*] destre devant le roi et son conseil a Westminstre,
et la le roi sanz encoupement ou encheson oustoit et remuoit
Hamound de Chigwelle, maire, de sa mairaute, et fist Nichol
de Farndoun gardein de la dit cite a la volunte le roi. Et le
dit Hamound de Chigwelle, Hamound Godechepe, Esmon
Lambyn (et: *interlined*) Roger Palmer, aldermans, siwerent la
court le roi ove grande doute pur attendre sa volente, et oier
ceo qil voilleit a eux dire, et de ceo qil les voleit acouper. En cel
temps apres la Trynite deux enfist miracles en la eglise de seint
Poel de Loundres a la table qe le dite counte de Lancastre aveit
fait pendre et peintre sur une piller, en remembrance qe le roi
avoit grantee et afferme les (les: *repeated*) ordinances. En cele
temps le roi fist lever le vj dener des biens en Loundres et en
altres citees, et le disme dener sur uppeland, en grant destresce
et enpoverisment del poeple de la terre. Cesti roi prist trewes
ovesqe les Escoz tanqe a la fine de xiij annz, sur diverses
condicions entre les parties affermez, si loiaute le voudre tenir.
En cele temps a la fest de seint Thomas la translacion lan xviij²⁵
comenceant, fust la dite table en la eglise de seint Poel, par bref
le roi de grant reddour ordeine, par une meistre Robert de
Baldok homme enginous et compassant de malveiste ouste, et
apres la cire qe illueqes fust offert en devocion del dite Thomas
de Lancastre. Meis ja pur ceo fust del tut ouste la devocion del
poeple qe oblacions ne furent faites al piler ou la dite table
pendoit, tant furent les miracles qe dieu overist pur le dite
Thomas overtz et publiez, qe multz des gentz se loioient de li.
Et le roi fist mettre gardeins et gaites, et fist cloer les huys del
eglise de Pountfreit oue le dit Thomas gisoit enterre, qe nul ne
poeit a li venire pur devocion faire, ne pur grant gent y venoit
de totes partez la terre tanqe a Pountfreit, et la donerent ils lour
oblacions a povres gentz en lonur de dieu et del dit Thomas.
Donqe avint issint meisme

---

²⁵ *Recte* xvii; and see Bodleian Library MS Lyell 17, fo. 115v.

(fo. 257)

aldermen summoned to be present before the king and his council at Westminster, and there the king, without indictment or cause, ousted and removed Hamo Chigwell, the mayor, from his mayoralty and appointed Nicholas Farndon keeper of the said city at the king's pleasure. And the aldermen, the said Hamo Chigwell, Hamo Godechepe, Edmund Lambyn, and Roger Palmer, followed the king's court in great fear to await upon his pleasure and hear what he wished to say to them and of what he wanted to accuse them. At this time, after Trinity Sunday [22 May], God performed miracles in the church of St Paul of London at the board which the said earl of Lancaster had had painted and hung on a pillar, in memory of the fact that the king had granted and established the Ordinances. At this time the king levied the sixth penny on goods in London and in other cities and the tenth penny on the countryside to the great distress and impoverishment of the people of the land. This king made truces with the Scots on various conditions established between the parties to last for thirteen years, provided they kept the conditions faithfully. At this time at the feast of the translation of St Thomas at the beginning of the [seventeenth] year [3 or 7 July],[26] the said board in St Paul's church, was removed by a certain master Robert Baldock, a false and evilly inclined man, on the most express instructions of the king, and subsequently the wax that was offered there in devotion of the said Thomas of Lancaster [was removed]. But although the people's devotion was entirely removed, so that offerings were not made at the pillar where the said board hung, such were the miracles that God worked for the said Thomas overtly and publicly that many people attached themselves to him. And the king had keepers and guards put in, and had the doors of the church of Pontefract where the said Thomas lay buried closed, so that no one might come to him to make devotion, for a great many people were coming from all parts of the land to Pontefract and there gave their offerings to poor people in honour of God and the said Thomas. Next, it so happened in the same year

---

[26] 3 July (Thomas the Apostle) or 7 July (Thomas Becket); the year was 1323.

(fo. 257v)

lan qe sire Roger de Mortumer seignur de Wygemore eschapa
hors de la Toure de Loundres a nuyt en la fest de seint Piere ad
vincula. Enquele maner il eschapa diverse parlance y fust, qar
ascuns gentz disoient qil eschapa par my une boure sotilement
fait qe fu done meisme le soire a les gaites de la Tour et as
altres, par quei ceux feurent le mieultz endormitz, et ascuns
disoient qil eschapa parmy une eschele de cordes enginousement
fait, la quele fust monstre lendemain as plusours de la Toure,
et ascuns disoient qil passa par my les portes de la dit Tour. Et
en cel temps qil eschapa il sen fuist tantqe a Porcestre, et illueqes
il se mist hastivent en mier et passa outre en la poer le counte
de Henaud. Et a ceo qe homme adonqe disoit, lettres furent
venuz del dite roi qe le dite sire Roger dust aver este traigne et
pendu dedeinz le quart jour apres, sil eust demure en la dite
Toure. Den apres en cele temps les quatre citeins de Loundres
qavoient siwi la court le roi en grant poour daver este destruit
come de sus est dit, revindrent a Loundres ove bele compaignie
des gentz lendemain de la exaltacion de la seinte croiz. En cel
temps a la feste de seint Martyn furent les citeins de Loundres
et gentz dautres villes attachez par une clerk qavoit a noum
Thomas de Neubyggynge qavoit purchace la commission le
(le: *repeated*) roi, lequel clerk mist sour les bones gentz qils
avoient parle ove le dit sire Roger de li maintenir et sustenire
dela la meer, et qe eux furent aidauntz et conseillauntz qil fust
eschape hors de la dit Tour de Loundres, de quele surmise les
bones gentz (les bones: *repeated*) les espurgerent par tote manere
de lei devant les justices le roi, issint qe le clerk fust tenu faux et
mis en prisone. Tost apres al quaresme pernant le roi tint
parlement a Westminstre, et la il seisit en sa main touz les biens
et chateux qe levesqe de Hereford avoit, et li fist tote la
persecucion qil savoit issint qe a grante peine se poeit il tenire
sauf dedeinz la purceinte de les freres menours de Loundres, qil
neust este pris hors de saintuarie par le poer le roi, et ceo fu
lencheson qe

(fo. 257v)

that sir Roger Mortimer, lord of Wigmore, escaped from the
Tower of London at night on the feast of St Peter ad Vincula
[1 August]. There were various accounts of how he escaped,
for some people said that he escaped by means of a cunningly
concocted drink which was given the same evening to the
guards of the Tower and to others, thanks to which they were
soundly put to sleep; some said he escaped by an ingeniously
made rope-ladder which was shown the next day to several
people in the Tower; still others said that he walked through
the doors of the said Tower. And when he escaped he fled to
Porchester and there he speedily put to sea and went abroad
into the lordship of the count of Hainault. And according to
what was then said, letters had come from the said king that
the said sir Roger was to be drawn and hanged within four
days if he had remained in the Tower. Subsequently, at this
time, the four citizens of London, who had followed the king's
court in great fear of being destroyed, as has been stated above,
returned to London with a handsome company of people the
day after the Exaltation of the Holy Cross [15 September]. At
this time, at the feast of St Martin [10 or 11 November] the
citizens of London and the people of other towns had been
charged by a clerk named Thomas Newbiggin who had
purchased the king's commission. This clerk accused the good
people of having spoken with the said sir Roger about
maintaining and supporting him to go abroad, and of having
aided and abetted his escape from the Tower of London, from
which accusation the good people cleared themselves by every
manner of legal procedure before the king's justices, so that
the clerk was held to be a liar and put in prison. Soon after at
Lent the king held parliament at Westminster and there he took
into his hands all the goods and chattels that the bishop of
Hereford possessed, and instituted against him all manner of
persecution that he could, so that only with great difficulty
could he [the bishop] find safety within the precinct of the
Greyfriars of London, with the result that he was not seized
from sanctuary by the royal power. And the pretext on which

(fo. 258)

le roi lui mist sour, qil avoit herberge les deux Mortumers et les counseille de maintenere lour partie encountre li. Mes la clergie li aida donqe en sa querele. Ensement le roi fist grante persecucion a sire William de Ayremynne evesqe de Norwiz et lui tint pur traitre, et si fust il tenu bone homme qi grauntment avoit travaille pur lestat du roialme. Auxi fist il grant duresce a sire Alisaundre de Bikenore ercevesqe de Divelyn.

Lan Mille CCCXXV[27] a la feste de seint Johan le Baptistre sourdist une grande descord entre le roi de Fraunce et le roi Dengleterre, pur homage nient fait pur la terre de Gascoigne, par quei le roi de Fraunce se corucea malement, et manda sa gent en Gascoigne pur seiser la terre en sa maine. Et le roi Dengleterre a la goule daugst apres fist assembler moltz des gentz armez a Portesmuthe, pur avere passe dela la meer a defendre les parties de Gascoigne. Et quant eux estoient venuz a Portesmuthe, la volente le roi chaungea, et ne les voleit suffrire passir, issint qe chescune compaignie se retourna en son paiis demene sanz espleit faire. Et le roi a la seint Michel apres, en despit du roi de Fraunce, seisist en sa main totes les terres qe la roigne sa compaigne avoit en Engleterre, et il remua touz le fraunceis chivalers et esquiers, dames (dames: *deleted in red*) et damoisels[28] qi furent demurauntz ove la dit roigne, et ceo fu par le conseil de Hugh le Despenser avant dit, et de sire Walter de Stapiltoun evesqe Dexcestre adonqe tresorer le roi, et dun meistre Robert Baldok adonqe chaunceller le roi, qi touz avoient apres mal fin, les queux counseillers et autres, par lour malveis compassement et faux conseil, ordinerent entre eux qe la roigne deveroit passer en Fraunce pur faire acord entre les deux rois, si qele passa outre devant la Pasqe.

Lan Mille CCCXXVI[29] le counte de Garrenne, le counte Dathels, et autres grantz passerent a la feste de la seinte croice en Maii a Portesmuthe vers Gascoigne od cent neefs attirrez et estuffez des gentz et de vitailles, a queu passage les Loundreis maunderent au roi vij[xx]

[27] *Recte* CCCXXIV.
[28] The feminine form 'demoiseles', which makes better sense of the balance of the sentence, is given in Bodleian Library MS Lyell 17, fo. 116 and CUL MS Gg.1.15, fo. 188v.
[29] *Recte* CCCXXV.

(fo. 258)

the king accused him was that he had harboured the two
Mortimers and advised them to maintain their opposition to
him [the king]. But the clergy assisted him [the bishop] then in
his dispute. Similarly the king severely persecuted sir William
Ayremynne, bishop of Norwich, and considered him a traitor,
yet he was thought to be a good man who had worked very
hard for the estate of the realm. Also he put great pressure on
sir Alexander Bicknor, archbishop of Dublin.

In [1324] at the feast of St John the Baptist [24 June] there
arose a serious disagreement between the king of France and
the king of England over the homage which had not been paid
for the land of Gascony. The king of France was very angry
about this and ordered his people into Gascony to seize the
land into his hands. And on the following 1 August the king
of England had many armed men mustered at Portsmouth in
order to cross the sea to defend Gascony. And when they had
come to Portsmouth the king changed his mind and would not
let them cross, so that each company returned to its own region
without achieving anything. And the king, at the following
Michaelmas [29 September], in defiance of the king of France
took into his hand all the lands that the queen, his consort,
possessed in England and he removed all the French knights
and esquires, ladies and pages who were with the said queen
and this was [done] by the advice of Hugh Despenser previously
mentioned and of sir Walter Stapledon, bishop of Exeter, at
that time the king's treasurer, and of a certain master Robert
Baldock, then the king's chancellor, all of whom subsequently
came to a bad end. These counsellors and others by their evil
schemes and false counsel determined between them that the
queen should cross to France to make accord between the two
kings, so she went abroad before Easter [7 April].

In [1325] earl Warenne, the earl of Atholl, and other lords, at
the feast of the Holy Cross in May [3 May], crossed from
Portsmouth to Gascony with 100 ships equipped and furnished
with men and provisions, for which voyage the Londoners
sent the king 140

(fo. 258v)

hommes a pee bien armez. Apres cel temps a la feste de la decollacion de seint Johan le Babtistre, le roi demura a Dovorre par trois semaines pur ordiner son passage vers le roi de Fraunce et avoit maunde outre sez vitailles, chivaux, tresor, et ses purveours furent en les parties de la pur sa purveance faire. Et le roi meismes fut en alant vers la meer pur aver entre en neef qe fust tut apparaille de lui resceivre pur passer. Et sire Hugh le Despenser le ficz, qi grandment fu hai des plusours grantz seignurs de la terre, et auxi de tote la commun, fist grant dolour et se pleinont pitousement au roi et dit qe sil passat outre qil serroit mis a la mort en labsence de lui. Par my quele pleinte la volente le roi changea, et ne voleit en nul manere entrere la neef, meis demura a grant hounte et deshonure de lui meisme, qar rois et autres grantz seignurs par dela attenderent sa venue. Et le roi parmy son malveis conseil manda en son lieu sire Edward son ficz heire de la terre pur faire hommage au roi de Fraunce, et lenfaunt fu bien et noblement resceu del roi de Fraunce, et fu fait duk de Guyenne. Ore la roigne et son chier ficz son en le parties par dela et ne poient revenire a lour pleiser pur ascuns grosses destorbances qe lour grevoint, pur quei le roi les tint sez enemis, et fist crier en Loundres, qe nul homme fust si hardi de porter lettres de la roigne ne de son ficz vers les partis Dengleterre, et si nul homme le feit qil deveroit estre attache, et ensement celui a qi la lettre irroit, et quex fuissent amenez devant le roi et son conseil. En cel temps la roigne si demena grantment de doel et de dolour come dame qe eust son seignur perdu, et (sa: *interlined*) meisne engleis fust remue hors de sa court de la. Le roi en cel temps fist bien afforcere des vitailles la Tour de Loundres (et: *interlined*) autre chastels en la terre, pur ceo qil dotoit mult de la venue la roigne et dautres estranges en sa compaignie. En cel temps fust ordeigne qe lestaple de leins deveroit demurer en Engleterre. Et crie fust qe nul homme deveroit amenere hors de ceste terre nul fullingerthe, ne tasels. Mes toute cele ordinance ne tint pas

(fo. 258v)

well-armed footmen. After this time, at the feast of the Decollation of St John the Baptist [29 August], the king remained at Dover for three weeks to arrange his passage to the king of France, and had his provisions, horses, and treasure sent across, and his purveyors were also over there for the purpose of provisioning him. The king himself was on his way to the sea to go aboard a ship which was completely ready to receive him for his crossing. And sir Hugh Despenser, the son, who was greatly hated by several great lords of the land and also by all the commonalty, was very distressed and complained piteously to the king and said that if he [the king] crossed he would be put to death in his absence. In the course of this complaint the king's attitude changed, and he would not in any way board the ship but stayed behind, to his great shame and dishonour, for kings and other great lords were over there awaiting his arrival. And the king with his evil counsellors sent in his place sir Edward his son, heir of the land, to pay homage to the king of France; and the youth was well received with due honour to his noble rank by the king of France and was made duke of Guyenne. Now the queen and her dear son were overseas and might not return when they wanted to because of certain great obstacles which impeded them. For this reason the king regarded them as his enemies; and he had it proclaimed in London that no one should be so rash as to carry letters from the queen or his son into England and, if any person did so, that he, and similarly he to whom the letter went, would be arrested and they would be brought before the king and his council. At this time the queen's demeanour was one of mourning and grief, like a lady who has lost her lord, and her English household was removed from her court over there. The king at this time had the Tower of London and other castles in the land further reinforced with provisions because he greatly feared the arrival of the queen and other foreigners in her company. At this time it was decreed that the wool staple should remain in England. And it was proclaimed that no man should take out of this land any fuller's earth or teasels. But this whole ordinance achieved

(fo. 259)

esploit. En cel an en este fu grant secheresce en rivers et en fountaignes, issint qils avoient grante defaute dawe en plosours paiis, si qe plusours villes en la terre ardoient come la ville de Roystoun, labbe de Croxtoun, Wandelesworth et autres arsouns y furent pur defaute deawe douce. En cel temps la (la: *repeated*) meer surmontoit leawe de Thamise qe fust salee, par quei moltz des gentz se pleignoient de la cervoise qe fu salee. En cel temps a la feste de seint Margarete le roi fist crier qe nul gent frаunceis ne dust marchander en la terre ne venire en cestes parties, pur ceo qe le roi de Fraunce et la femme au roi Dengleterre, nient apelle roigne en la crie, et son eisne ficz furent encontre li, come sez enemis, furent en point daver este trahis en les parties de Fraunce, et aver este mandez en Engleterre par tresoun pur le grant avoir qe le roi et sire Hugh le Despenser le ficz et autres qi furent de lour acorde (aveient maunde)[30] a les xij piers de Fraunce, en grante desceivance de la dite roigne et son chier ficz sire Edward, par qei en cel temps touz les engleis qi adonqes furent el roialme de Fraunce furent attachez en une jour, qe amountoit a grant multitude de gentz. Quant la roigne et sire Edward son ficz aperceurent del compassement lour seignur et de ses malveis conseillers, ils procurent et attraierent a eux grant poer des gentz darmes et dautres, od grante navie devenir en Engleterre, par quei grant afforcement et gaite fu faite par terre et par meer, issint qe ala feste de la decollacion de seint Johan ceux de Loundres maunderent au roi au Porcestre cent hommes bien armez. Meisme cel an le mesqerdy prochein devant la seint Michel, cestassaver le iiij doctobre qe adonqe fust par lundy,[31] la roigne et son eisne ficz, sire Roger de Mortumer, sire Johan de Henaud et autres grantz ariverent a Herewyche en Suffolk, a destruire les enemis de la terre. Et si tost come eux furent arivez, le vent chaungea come dieu le voleit et lour neefs qi les amenerent en ceste terre sieglerent seins et sauf en les parties dount eles vinderent. Et quant la roigne et son eisne ficz feurent ainsi arivez, le paiis par tout de chescune part enviroun cheist a

---

[30] Ibid., fo. 116v.
[31] Michaelmas was indeed a Monday. *Cestassaver le iiij doctobre* is an erroneous insertion in the Anonimalle manuscript; see above p. 37.

(fo. 259)

nothing. In this year in summer there was a great drought in rivers and springs with the result that there was a great lack of water in many areas so that a number of towns in the land burned, like the town of Royston, the abbey of Croxton, Wandlesworth, and there were other fires for lack of fresh water. At this time the sea overwhelmed the water of the Thames which became saline. As a result many people complained of the ale which became salty. At this time at the feast of St Margaret [20 July], the king had it proclaimed that no French people might trade in the land nor come to these parts because the king of France and the wife of the king of England, not described as queen in the proclamation, and his eldest son were opposed to him. As his enemies, [they] were on the point of being betrayed in France and of being treacherously sent into England, because of the great treasure which the king and sir Hugh Despenser the son and others who were of their persuasion (had sent) to the twelve peers of France for the great undoing of the said queen and her dear son sir Edward. By this action all the English who were then in the realm of France were arrested in one day, which amounted to a great multitude of people. When the queen and sir Edward her son became aware of the plotting of their lord and his evil counsellors they raised and drew to themselves a great force of men at arms and others to come to England with a great navy. In response to this, great reinforcement was made and close watch was kept on land and at sea, so that at the feast of the Decollation of St John [29 August] the Londoners sent to the king at Porchester 100 well-armed men. The same year, on Wednesday next before Michaelmas [24 September], that is to say on 4 October which then was a Monday, the queen and her eldest son, sir Roger Mortimer, sir John of Hainault, and other lords arrived at Harwich in Suffolk in order to destroy the enemies of the land. And as soon as they had arrived the wind changed in accordance with God's will and their ships which brought them to this land sailed back safe and sound to the country from which they had come. And when the queen and her eldest son had thus arrived, the countryside everywhere around willingly went over to

(fo. 259v)

eux de bone volente, et ils maunderent lour lettres au maire et
a la communalte de Loundres, qeux fuissent aidantz en la querel
qe la roigne et sire Edward son ficz avoient commence, a
destruire les enemis de la terre, mes nul respouns ne fust a eux
maunde a cel foiz pur doute du roi et de les deux Despensers,
et autres qi adonqes furent a la Tour de Loundres, par quei la
roigne et son ficz maunderent une autre lettre a Loundres,
overte enseale de lour seals pendauntz, et fust fichi en laube de
jour sur la novele croice en Chepe en Loundres, et la copie de
la lettre fu fiche par aillours sur fenestres, qi plusours la poient
lire, et ceo fu le jeody en la feste de seint Dynys, qe les bons de
Loundres fuissent aidantz a destruire sire Hugh le Despenser et
autres enemis pur commun profit de tot le roialme, et qe la
comunalte lour deveroit sur ceo lour volente maunder. Par qei
multz des gentz ne savoient qei faire, oue de maintenire la
partie le roi et de sire Hugh le Dispenser, qi furent adonqe molt
mal compassantz, oue de tenire ove la roigne ou son ficz, qi
furent venuz en bone arraie pur la commun profist de la terre a
defaire les enemis. Ceo est la copie de la lettre.

Isabel[32] par la grace de Dieu roigne Dengleterre, dame
Dirlande, et countesse de Pountif, et nous Edward eisne
ficz au roi Dengleterre, duk de Guyenne, counte de Cestre,
de Pountif, et de Mounstroille, a tot la communalte de
Loundres, salutz. Come nous vous avoms autrefoiz mande
par noz lettres, coment nous sumes venuz en cest terre od
bon arraye et en bone manere pur lonur et le profist de
seint eglise et de nostre trescher seignur le roi et de tout le
roialme meintenire et garder a nostre poer demene, si
come nous et totes bones gentz du dit roialme sumes tenuz
affaire. Et sur ceo nous vous avoms prie par noz dites
lettres, qe vous nous soiez aidant taunt come vous purrez
on cest querele, qest pur le commun profist de tout le
roialme, et nous neioms uncore eu nul respouns des dites
lettres, ne ne savoms rien de vostre volente, si envoioms a
vous derichier, et nous mandoms et prioms, qe vous vous
portez issint devers nous, qe nous neioms cause de vous

---

[32] *Margin*: littera civitate Londoniense directa.

(fo. 259v)

them, and they sent their letters to the mayor and commonalty of London to the effect that they should help them in the cause that the queen and sir Edward her son had begun, to destroy the enemies of the land; but no reply was sent to them at this time for fear of the king and the two Despensers and others who were then at the Tower of London. Because of this the queen and her son sent another open letter to London sealed with their pendant seals, and it was fixed at dawn on the new cross in Cheapside in London, and copies of the letter were fixed elsewhere on windows so that greater numbers could read it, and this was on Thursday, the feast of St Denis [9 October]. It said that the good people of London should help to destroy sir Hugh Despenser and other enemies for the common profit of all the realm; and that the commonalty ought to make their will known on this. As a result many people did not know what to do, whether to support the side of the king and of sir Hugh Despenser, who were then planning much wickedness, or to hold with the queen and her son who had come in good order for the common profit of the land to destroy its enemies. This is the copy of the letter.

Isabella by the grace of God queen of England, lady of Ireland, and countess of Ponthieu, and we, Edward, eldest son of the king of England, duke of Guyenne, earl of Chester, Ponthieu, Montreuil, to all the commonalty of London, greetings. As we have formerly told you by our letters, how we have come to this land in good order and with good intent for the honour and profit of Holy Church and of our very dear lord the king and to uphold and safeguard all the realm with our own might, as we and all good people of the said realm are bound to do; and as on this we have asked you by our said letters to help us as much as you can in this cause which is for the common profit of all the realm; and as we have still not had any reply to the said letters nor do we know anything of your will, we therefore send to you again. And we ask and pray that you will so behave towards us that we will not have reason

E

(fo. 260)

grever. Meis qe vous nous soiez aidant par totes les voies qe vous saurez et porrett, et tutefoiz qe nous vous emprieroms ou qe vous verrez lieu et temps, qar soiez certaine qe nous et touz ceuz qi sount venuz odvesqe nous en ceste terre ne pensoms affaire ne ne ferroms, si dieu plest, chose qe ne serra pur le commun profist de la terre, sauve a destruire sire Hugh le Despenser nostre enemie et a tote le roialme, si come vous bien savez, par quei nous vous prioms et chargeoms sur la foi qe vous devez a nostre seignur le roi et a nous, sur quant qe vous purrez[33] devers nous, qi si le dit Hugh le Dispenser nostre enemy viegne dedeinz vostre poer, qe vous lui facez hastivement prendre et sauvement garder, taunt qe nous eoms ordene de lui nostre volente. Et ceo ne lessez en nul manere si come vous desirez honur et profite de nous touz et de tout le roialme. Et si vous le faitz, sachez qe nous vous seroms touz jours le mieultz tenuz, et si engaignerez assetz donour et de profist de nous, si nous remandez hastivement tote vostre volente. Done a Baldok le vj jour doctobre.

Den apres avint issint qe lendemain qe la dit lettre fu venue a Loundres, come devant est dist, le roi meisme, Hugh Despenser, meistre Robert de Baldok et autres ove grant compaignie des gentz darmes se remuerent hors de la Tour de Loundres devers les parties de Bristut. Et les gentz de Loundres conseilerent entre eux quele chose ils voleient faire, et quele respouns ils voleient doner au dite roine et a son ficz, issint qe les coers dascuns gentz furent grantement engrossez, qils ne savoient qei faire ne qei dire ne quele respouns doner. Et sur ceo Hamond de Chigewelle adonqe maire de la dite citee, et les viscountes, et les aldermans de la dite citee furent esluz devant monsire Geffrey Lescrope, monsire Walter de Norwiz, et monsire Hervy de Staunton et autres du prive conseil le roi, a les freres prechoures de Loundres, le mesqerdy procheine devant la feste de seint Luk, qe adonqe fu par une samadi, dount grante parlance y fust entre plusours de la commun, qei cele prive counseil fust illoeqe, et sucheront qe ceo fu pur mal et en desceivance de la cite, issi qe ascuns

[33] The copy of the letter in the Plea and Memoranda roll adds 'forfaire' here (London Record Office, Plea and Memoranda Roll A 1b, fo. 10), as do Bodleian Library MS Lyell 17, fo. 117v and CUL MS Gg.1.15, fo. 191v.

(fo. 260)

to harm you – but that you should be helpful to us in every way you know how and can be, and at every time that we ask it of you, or that you see an opportunity; for be sure that we and all those who have come with us to this land do not intend to do, and, please God, will not do, anything which will not be for the common profit of the land, save to destroy sir Hugh Despenser, our enemy and all the realm's, as you well know. Because of this we beg you and charge you on the faith which you owe to our lord the king and to us, considering what you might [forfeit] to us, that if the said sir Hugh Despenser our enemy should come within your power that you should have him taken quickly and kept safely until we have indicated our will with him. And do not neglect this in any way, as you desire the honour and profit of us all and of all the realm. And if you do this, know that we will be always the more bound to you, and so you will gain very great honour and profit from us. Therefore send quickly to tell us all your will. Given at Baldock, 6th October.

Then afterwards, the day after the said letter had come to London, as is described above, the king himself, Hugh Despenser, master Robert Baldock, and others with a great company of men at arms moved from the Tower of London towards Bristol. And the Londoners discussed among themselves what they should do and what reply they wanted to give to the said queen and her son, with the result that the hearts of some of the people were greatly troubled, so that they did not know what to do or say nor what reply to give. And concerning this, Hamo Chigwell, then mayor of the said city, and the sheriffs and the aldermen of the said city were chosen before Geoffrey Lescrope, sir Walter of Norwich, and sir Hervy Staunton and others of the king's privy council at the Blackfriars of London on Wednesday next before the feast of St Luke [15 October] which was then on a Saturday; there was much talk about this matter among a number of the commonalty as to why this privy council was there and they thought that this was for evil doing and in deceit of the city. Accordingly some

(fo. 260v)

persones de la commune sasemblerent et encountrerent le maire
et la resonerent de gros coer, et qil ne deveroit tiel prive conseil
tenir hors de la Gihale, par quei le maire en grante doute sen ala
ovesqe eux a la Gihale, et parlerent entre eux de ceux qi furent
enemis la roigne et a la cite. Et monstre fust qe sire Walter de
Stapeltoun evesqe Dexcestre fust une des enemis la roigne, qi
lavoit mis a sez gages de xx sous le jour. Et quant Johan le
Mareschal fust espie le dit sire Hugh le Despenser et altres
persones dount tost apres crie fust en Chepe, qe les enemis le
roi deveroient tost voider la ville; ne demura gairs apres qe le
dit Johan le Mareschal fu pris entour le middi de meisme le
mesqerdy, en son hostel, pur tiele come il fust tenue, et mene
en Chepe, despoille, confesse, et decole, et ascuns persones
meisme le hure alerent al hostel le dit evesqe Dexcestre de hors
la barre du temple, pur rifler le dite hostel. Et le dit evesqe qe
fu venu de Enefeld avoit entendu en Holeburn qe tiels gentz
furent a son hostel avant dit, et quida aver en sauf refust a
Loundres, et chivaucha a raundoun par my Neugate et derere
la bocherie tantqe a la glise de seint Poel. Et quant il fust pres al
entre del huis devers le north il fust encountre, et hape de tutes
partz, et tost deschivauche, mene en Chepe, despoille, et decole,
et deux de sez esquiers, lun avoit a noum William Atte Walle et
lautre Johan de Padyngtoun, furent meisme le jour decolez.
Ore est la citee de Loundres leve odvesqe la roigne et sire
Edward son ficz, et fount a eux jurer evesqes, abbes, priours,
countes, barouns, et autres grantz de la terre a vivre et murir
ovesqe eux en la querele comence. Et ceux qi furent emprisonez
en la Tour de Loundres pur la querele dount le gentil counte
monsire Thomas de Lancastre murust, ceux de Loundres les
fist deliverer. Denapres quant le roi avoit entendu de ceo qe fu
fait par ceux de Loundres et ales autres en sa compaignie se
tindrent abaiz et la roigne et son ficz et lor compaignie

(fo. 260v)

persons of the commonalty assembled together and met with
the mayor and argued strongly that he should not hold such a
privy council outside the Guildhall. Because of this the mayor,
in great fear, went with them to the Guildhall and they discussed
between themselves who were the enemies of the queen and
the city. And it was demonstrated that sir Walter Stapledon,
bishop of Exeter, who had put her on a wage of 20 shillings a
day was one of the Queen's enemies. Soon after it was
proclaimed in Cheapside that the king's enemies should quickly
leave town, and since John the Marshal was a spy of the said sir
Hugh Despenser and other persons, the said John the Marshal,
being considered such an enemy, was seized not long after in
his lodgings, at about midday on the same Wednesday, and led
into Cheapside, stripped, confessed and beheaded. Some at the
same hour went to the lodging of the said bishop of Exeter
outside Temple Bar to plunder the said lodging. The said
bishop, who had come from Enfield, had heard in Holborn
that such people were at his aforesaid lodging and he thought
he would have safe refuge in London, and rode swiftly through
Newgate and behind the Butchery as far as the church of St
Paul's. When he was near the entrance of the north door he
was met and seized from all sides and quickly unhorsed, led to
Cheapside, stripped, and beheaded, and two of his esquires,
one called William Attewelle and the other John Paddington,
were beheaded on the same day. Now the city of London rose
with the queen and sir Edward her son, and made bishops,
abbots, priors, earls, barons and other lords of the land swear
to them to live and die with them in the cause which had now
begun. And as for those who were imprisoned in the Tower of
London in connection with the cause in which the noble earl,
sir Thomas Lancaster had died, the Londoners had them freed.
When the king had heard what had been done by the Londoners
[he] and others in his company were astonished and the queen
and her son and their company

(fo. 261)

bien paiez. Le roi en la compaignie de sez enemis sen fuist de la compaignie la roigne, et ele lui pursiwist de li aver ouste de sez enemis, et de rejoier son seignur si ele poeit. Meis le roi ne voleit lesser la compaignie de sez enemis. Meis il se mist en eawe a Bristut et voleit aver passe en Irlande, meis par force de vent il fust chace en Gales, et passuit avant qomme ne savoit adonqe oue le roi estoit devenuz, meis sire Hugh le Despenser le piere se tint el chastel de Bristut, et illueqes fust il pris. Et le lundy en la velle des apostres seint Symond et seint Jude, il fust trayne, pendu, et decole illueqes, et sa teste maunde a Wyncestre pur ceo qil estoit counte de Wyncestre. En cel temps le dymange a nuyt cestassaver en la feste de seint Esmon lerevesqe [sic], et cel jour fu merveillous tonoir en queu temps monsire Henry de Lancastre et autres guntz [sic] pursiwerent les enemis le roi enginousement dun part et dautre en les parties de Gales a Snawedoun prede labbeie de Northe [sic] si estreitement, qe le roi guerpist ses enemis et se tint a sez leges gentz, et les enemis furent pris, cestassaver Hugh le Despenser le ficz, meis [sic] Robert de Baldok, et altres remenez en Engleterre a Hereford od grante hounte et hu et crie. Et avant qils vindrent a Hereford le counte Darundelle fust decole illueqes, cestassaver le lundy lendemain de la feste seint Esmon lercevesqe. Et le lundy en la veille de seinte Katerine fu le dit sire Hugh le Despenser trayne, pendu, et decole, sez boels ars, et quartrone a Hereford. Et une Symond de Redyngges, qavoit despise la roigne, illueqes traigne et pendu. Et le dit mestre Robert de Baldok, qestoit chanceller le roi et homme enginous, fu mis en prison levesqe de Hereford. Et le joedy apres manger cestassaver la surveille de seint Nicholas fu la teste al dit sire Hugh porte a Loundres od trumpes par my Chepe, et la test fiche sur le pounte de Loundres. En cel temps le roi fust el chastel de Kenilworth en la compaignie le dit counte de Lancastre, et la roigne

(fo. 261)

were well avenged. The king in the company of his enemies
fled from the queen's company; she pursued him in order to
have him removed from his enemies and in order to rejoin her
lord if she could. But the king would not leave the company of
his enemies. He took to the water at Bristol and wished to
cross to Ireland but he was driven into Wales by a strong wind
and crossed there before anyone knew therefore where the king
had arrived. Sir Hugh Despenser the father stayed in Bristol
castle and there he was captured. On Monday, the eve of the
feast of the Apostles Saints Simon and Judas [27 October], he
was drawn, hanged and beheaded at that place and his head
was sent to Winchester because he was earl of Winchester. At
this time, on Sunday night, that is to say on the feast of St
Edmund the archbishop [16 November], and during the day,
there was marvellous thunder, during which time sir Henry of
Lancaster and other great men pursued the king's enemies
cleverly from one place to another at Snowdon in Wales near
to Neath Abbey, so closely that the king left his enemies and
joined his liege people and the enemies were captured, that is
to say Hugh Despenser the son, master Robert Baldock and
others, and were brought back into England at Hereford with
great shame and hue and cry. As soon as they came to Hereford
the earl of Arundel was beheaded there, that is to say on
Monday after the feast of St Edmund the archbishop [17
November]. And on Monday the eve of St Katherine [24
November], at Hereford the said sir Hugh Despenser was
drawn, hanged and beheaded, his bowels burnt, and quartered.
And there a certain Simon of Reading who had insulted the
queen was drawn and hanged. The said master Robert Baldock
who was the king's chancellor and a wily man was put in the
Bishop of Hereford's prison. On Thursday after dinner, that is
to say two days before the feast of St Nicholas [4 December],
the head of the said sir Hugh was carried to London through
Cheapside accompanied by trumpets, and the head was impaled
on London Bridge. At this time the king was at Kenilworth
castle with the said earl of Lancaster. The queen

(fo. 261v)

et son eisne ficz tindrent lour Noel a Walyngford. Et la vint a li
son ficz sire Johan de Eltham ove bele compaignie des gentz de
Loundres, qi lamenerent a la roigne, pur ceo qil estoit adonqe
en la garde de la cite. En cel men temps Hughelyn le Despenser
ficz au dist sire Hugh se tint el chastel de Kerfily. En cel temps
nul bref de roi fu maunde en la terre fors depar la roigne et de
sire Edward son eisne ficz. Et la roigne et sire Edward son ficz
vindrent a Loundres ov ben compaignie des gentz le dymanche
procheine devant la feste de la Typhayne pur tenire parlement,
issint qe le mardy, cest (a dir: *interlined*) en la feste de seint
Hiller, lercevesqe de Caunterbury pronuncia a Westminstre
devant le poeple plusours articles encountre le roi, par quei le
poeple graunta et cria qil ne deveroit plus reigner, meis qe son
fice duk de Guyenne seroit roi; pur quei evesqes, abbes, priours,
countes, barouns, chivalers, et burgeis furent maundez au roi
al dit chastel de Kenilworth pur rendre a li sus homage et pur
saver sil voleit assentire al corounement de son ficz, et il
assentist qar il ne poeit autrement estre, et fu lour homage
rendu a li par monsire William Trussell, qi adonqe fust fet lour
procuratour, en cestes paroles:

> Jeo William Trussell procuratour des prelatz, countes, ba-
> rons, et autres gentz nomez en ma procuracie, eiaunt a
> ceo pleine et suffisance poer, les homages et les feautes a
> vous Edward roi Dengleterre avant ces hures faites par les
> persones en ma dite procuracie nomez, en noum de touz
> et de chescune de eux par certeines causes en ma dite
> procuracie contenuz, renk et rebaille sus a vous, dit
> Edward, et delivre et face quites les persones avantdites
> en la meilloure manere qe lei ou custume donne. Et face
> protestacion en noum de eux qils ne voleient desore
> enavant en vostre feaute nen vostre ligeaunce estre, ne ne
> cleiment de vous come du roi riens a tenire, einz vous
> teignent ore persone privez sanz nul manere de real dignite.

Et tant[34] come les grauntz ove lour procuratour furent illueqes
parler ove le roi, si fu crie en Chepe, qe touz ceux qi devoient
seute oue service au roi, qils fuissent al corounement del novel
roi le dymanche en la veille de la Chaundeleure,

---

[34] 'ore persone . . . Et tant' supplied in margin.

(fo. 261v)

and her eldest son kept their Christmas at Wallingford. And her son, sir John of Eltham, came to her there with a fine company of Londoners who brought him to the queen because he was at that time in the safe-keeping of the City. At this time Hughlyn Despenser, the son of the said sir Hugh, remained in Caerphilly castle. In this period no writ of the king was sent into the land save by the queen and by sir Edward her eldest son. The queen and sir Edward her son came to London together with a good company of people on the Sunday next before the feast of Epiphany [4 January], in order to hold parliament. Therefore on Tuesday, that is to say on the feast of St Hilary [13 January], at Westminster the archbishop of Canterbury read out before the people several articles against the king. Because of this the people agreed and cried out that he should no longer reign, but that his son the duke of Guyenne should be king; therefore certain bishops, abbots, priors, earls, barons, knights and burgesses were sent to the king at the said Kenilworth castle to give back to him their homage and to find out whether he would assent to the coronation of his son. He agreed for he could not do otherwise, and their homage was returned to him in these words by sir William Trussell who was made their proctor at that time:

I, William Trussell, proctor of the prelates, earls, barons, and other people named in my procuracy, having by this full and sufficient power, render and give back to you the said Edward the homages and fealties made to you Edward, king of England, before this time by the persons named in my said procuracy, in the name of all and each of them, for certain causes contained in my procuracy, and release and make quit the persons aforesaid in the best way that law and custom allow. And I make a solemn affirmation in their name that they do not wish henceforth to be in your fealty nor your liegeance nor to admit themselves as holding anything from you as king, but rather they hold you now as a private person with no manner of royal dignity.

And while the lords with their proctor were there to speak with the king, it was proclaimed in Cheapside that all those who owed suit or service to the king should be at the coronation of the new king on Sunday the eve of Candlemas [1 February],

(fo. 262)

et trestouz vindrent al comandement (le roi et coronerent: *added in right margin*) sire Edward le eisne (ficz: *added in left margin*) a Westminstre ove grant joie et od grant honur, et naveit qe xiiij annz dage le jour de seint Bryce devant. Quant cesti Edward estoit coroune le dimanche en la veille de la Chaundeleure come devaunt est dit, il tint parlement a Westminstre, en quel parlement le roi granta a les citezeines de Loundres totes lour fraunchises avant perdues et autres fraunchises de novel. Et ceux qi furent pris dedeinz la fraunchise pur larcin felonie deveroient estre juggez devant le maire en la Gyhale de Loundres, par quei le utisme jour furent trois juggez a la mort et penduz, qe adonqe fu le venderdy prochein apres la feste de seint Johan ante portam latinam. En cel temps le roi piere a cesti novel roi fu remue hors du chastel de Kenilworth jesqes al chastel de Berkeleye, pur ceo qe grant parlaunce y fust parmy la terre qe ascuns coviegnes y feurent faites de plusours, pur li aver pris a force hors du dit chastel de Kenilworth, et qe frere Thomas Dunheved frere prechour et bon clerk fust assentu od coveignes dascunes freres del ordre, par quei il et autres furent emprisonez a Everwyk. Avint isint tost apres qe la roi eu maladist illueqes et murust le jour de seint Matheu le apostre devant le seint Michel, et fust enterre a Gloucestre en la veille de seint Thomas, quant il avoit regne xix annz, trois mois et deux semaines, de qi alme dieu ait merci amen. *En cel temps il y avoit grant descord entre le pape Johan et monsire Lowiz duk de Baver, qi fust eslu emperour de Rome, encountre qi le pape sovent envoia fort host et puissant pur li destruire. Meis sire Lowiz les enchacea arere hors del empire, et prist totes les citees et villes qui furent appurtenances al dite empire en Lumbardie, et par force les occupa, et auxi prist il tut le tresor le pape Johan. Cesti pape Johan molt pursiwist lordre des freres menours.*

Lan de grace Mille CCCXXVII la clergie de la les mountz et le poeple de Rome, ove le duk de Baver le quel ils avoient fet emperour come devant est dit, lavant dit pape Johan a Rome publierent heretik, et qil dust estre

(fo. 262)

and they all came at the king's command and crowned sir Edward his eldest son at Westminster with great joy and with great honour. He was only fourteen years old on the previous feast of St Brice [13 November]. When this Edward had been crowned, on Sunday the eve of Candlemas as was aforesaid, he held parliament at Westminster, in which parliament the king granted to the citizens of London all their franchises [which had been] formerly lost and other new franchises. [It was granted that] those who were taken within the franchise for larceny and felony should be judged before the mayor in the Guildhall of London and for this reason on the eighth day three were sentenced to death and to hang, this was on the Friday next after the feast of St John ante Portam Latinam [8 May]. At this time, the king, father to this new king, was removed from Kenilworth to Berkeley castle because there was great rumour throughout the land that some plots had been made by certain individuals to have him taken by force from the said Kenilworth castle, and that brother Thomas Dunheved, a Dominican and a good clerk, had agreed to the plots of some friars of the order, on account of which he and the others were imprisoned at York. It so happened that soon afterwards the king became ill there and died on the day of St Matthew the Apostle before Michaelmas [21 September], and was buried at Gloucester on the eve of St Thomas [20 December], after he had reigned nineteen years, three months and two weeks, on whose soul may God have mercy, Amen. At this time there was great discord between the pope John and sir Louis duke of Bavaria who had been elected emperor of Rome, against whom the pope more than once sent a strong and powerful army in order to destroy him. But sir Louis drove them back from the empire, and took all the cities and towns which belonged to the said empire in Lombardy and occupied them by force, and also he took all pope John's treasure. This pope John greatly harassed the Franciscan Order.

In the year of grace 1327 the ultramontane clergy and the people of Rome together with the duke of Bavaria, whom they had made emperor as was said above, proclaimed at Rome the aforesaid pope John to be a heretic and that he should be

(fo. 262v)

ouste de droit de cele dignite. Et pur ceo ils fesoient pape a Rome une frere menour, Peres de Corvarie, et li nomerent Nichol le quint. Adonqe le pape Johan pursiwist ascuns del dit ordre, dount freres Michel de Sezerie general ministre de meisme lordre et William de Okham Dengleterre grant clerk alerent en Baver pur trier la cause, les queux la pape voleit aver dampne, et pur ceo ils fuirent al emperour.

Edward avoit de sa femme

Edward le tierce apres le conqueste	Johan qi fu counte de Cornewaille	Alianore qe fu done au counte de Gerle	Johanne qe fu done a David roi Descoce

Ore regna le roi Edward le tiers puis le conquest bien et noblement, lan de grace avantdite, et ad grante et afferme tieles fraunchises a les citezeines de Loundres qonqes (le: *deleted*) roi devant son temps ne granta. En cel temps a la Pentecoste apres, le roi saparailla daler sur ses enemis Descoce ove tote le poer qil poeit a lui attrere, et od bele compaignie de Hanautz, par quei ceux de Loundres maunderent au roi a la goule daugst viij^{xx} hommes a chival bien armeez. En cel temps a Everwyk les Hanautz oscirent nutaundre moltz des Engleis, adonqe furent les Escoz entrez el park de Stanhope en Engleterre. Et le roi od son poer vint illueqe, et demura bien xv jours, et quei par envie qe les (les: *repeated*) grauntz avoient devers les Henautz, et que par fausine et compassement dascuns grantz de la terre, les Escoz eschaperent hors del dit park, la oue ils poeient aver este pris, confounduz, et occis, et sen alerent en lour paiis demene a graunte hounte, vileinie, et despit de tote Engleterre, qe les Escoz si legerement eschaperent hors del poer Dengleterre. Et a ceo qe commune parlaunce adonqe fust, sire James Douglas Descoz passa par my lost Dengleterre pres del pavilloun le roi, pur lui avere ravi en le

(fo. 262v)

justly removed from that dignity. And because of that they made a Franciscan, Peter of Corvara, pope in Rome and named him Nicholas V. Consequently the pope John pursued certain members of the said order, from whom brothers Michael of Cesena, minister general of the same order, and William of Ockham of England, a great clerk, went into Bavaria to judge the dispute; these the pope sought to have condemned and because of that they fled to the emperor.

Edward had by his wife

Edward III after the conquest	John who was earl of Cornwall	Eleanor who was married to the count of Guelderland	Jeanne who was married to David, king of Scotland

Now the king Edward, the third since the conquest, reigned well and nobly in the year of grace aforesaid, and granted and confirmed franchises to the citizens of London such as no king before his time had ever granted. At this time at Pentecost following [31 May], the king prepared to proceed against his Scottish enemies with all the force which he could muster and with a handsome company of Hainaulters, for which [campaign] the Londoners sent to the king 160 well-armed horsemen on 1 August. At this time at York the Hainaulters killed many of the English at night. Then the Scots entered the park of Stanhope in England, and the king with his forces came there and stayed a good fifteen days, and because of the jealousy that the lords felt towards the Hainaulters and because of the deception and the conspiracy of certain of the lords of the land the Scots escaped from the said park where they could have been captured, utterly defeated, and killed, and went away into their own country to the great shame, injury and contempt of all England, that the Scots escaped so lightly from England's might. And according to rumour, sir James Douglas of Scotland had at that time passed through the English army near to the king's pavilion intending to snatch him away into the

(fo. 263)

poer Descoz. Et le dit sire James eschapa, meis une chapeleyn arme qi fust vigerous homme fust arrestuz et occis. Tost apres le roi et les soens retournerent en Engleterre. Et maintenant les Escoce vindrent autrefoicz en ceste terre od grandesme ost ardant, robbant, et destruant, et fesoient molt des maux, tanqe ils vindrent al chastel de Alnewyk, oue monsire Henry de Percy adonqe estoit, et lui assegerent. Meis par force ils furent enchacez du dit chastel, et ils alerent dillueqe et assegerent le chastel de Werkworth, oue les Escoz perdirent graunt nombre de lour gentz. Et issint sanz nul esplait ils retournerent en lour paiis demene. Dens apres meisme cel an, dame Philippe la fille le counte de Henaut vint en Engleterre destre marie a monsire Edward le joefne roi corounee, et ele vint a Loundres la surveille de Noel, ou ele fust joiousement resceu des citezeins de la citee. Et ele fust espose a Everwyk le dymanche en la conversion de seint Poel.

Lan mille CCCXXVIII le roi tint parlement a Everwyk, a quel parlement les messagers Descoz vindrent pur treter de la pees. Et apres le roi maunda de sez messages en Escoce pur meisme lencheson, issint qe parmy lour ordinance dune part et dautre, la pees fu crie et publie entre les deux roialmes, et qe David le ficz sire Robert de Bruis esposeroit dame Johane de la Tour la soer au dit roi Dengleterre. En cel temps le dymanche procheine devant la feste de seint Margarete qe adonqe fu par meskerdy, David le ficz Robert de Bruys appelle roi Descoz joefne enfant esposa dame Johane de la Tour (*the above passage from* la soer au dit roi Dengleterre *to* Johane de la Tour *is repeated; it then continues*) la file le roi Edward de Caernavan [*sic*], issi qe par my celes esposailles furent renduz au dit sire David, ficz et heire le dit sire Robert de Bruys, le roialme Descoce ov totes ses droitures, et fraunchises, custumes, et la lettre qe fu appelle

(fo. 263)

power of Scotland. And the said sir James escaped but an armed chaplain who was a stalwart man was caught and killed. Soon after this, the king and his men returned to England. Now the Scots came again into this land with a very great army, burning, robbing, and destroying and did much harm, until they came to Alnwick castle where sir Henry Percy was [residing] and besieged him. But they were driven away by force from the said castle and went from there and besieged Warkworth castle where the Scots lost a great number of their men. And so, with nothing achieved, they returned to their own country. After that, in the same year, lady Philippa, the daughter of the count of Hainault, came to England to be married to sir Edward the young king, who had been crowned. She came to London two days before Christmas [23 December], where she was joyously received by the citizens of the city. And she was married at York on Sunday, the Conversion of St Paul [25 January, 1328].

In 1328 the king held parliament at York, to which parliament messengers came from Scotland to treat of peace. And afterwards the king sent his messages into Scotland for the same reason, so that, through negotiation on both sides, peace was declared and publicised between the two realms; and [it was declared] that David the son of sir Robert Bruce would marry lady Jeanne of the Tower, sister of the said king of England. At this time, on the Sunday before the feast of St Margaret which was then on a Wednesday [17 July], David the son of Robert Bruce, who was described as the young king of Scotland, married lady Jeanne of the Tower, daughter of the king, Edward of Caernarvon. The result was that through these nuptials the realm of Scotland with all its rights and franchises and customs, and the letter which was called

(fo. 263v)

Ragement, ove les seales del homage fait au noble roi Edward ael le roi quore est et a sez heires. Et issint sont les Escoz plenement delivres hors de la seignurie, et du service, et de chescune manere de droit due au roi Dengleterre et a sez heirs a touz jours. En cel temps la roigne la mere al novel roi et sire Roger de Mortumer acrocherent a eux roial poer et le tresor du roialme, et tindrent le roi de south lour subiection, et firent tant qe monsire Henre counte de Lancastre, qe fu fait al corounement le roi par commun assent du roialme son chef gardein, qil ne poeit a lui aprocher, counseiller, ne garder, par quei le counte ovesqe son counseille et dascuns grantz du roialme, et par my le counseil meistre Symond de Mepham, qi adonqe estoit ercevesqe de Canterbirs, et autres evesqes, se moveint devers la partie, pur redrescer la defaute, et qe le roi poeit vivre come roi del son sanz torcenouses prises faire enpoverissement de son poeple, par quei parlement fust ordeine a Salesbirs. Meis nul fust tenu, par quei les parties furent en point daver entreferue sure le pleine de Salesbirs, meis ceo fu destourbe par le conseil dascuns graunz, et fu parlement adonqe ordene a la Chaundeleure.

Lan Mille CCCXXIX a la feste de seint Hiller, le roi par my le conseil sa mere et le Mortumer dune part, et le dit monsire Henry counte de Lancastre dautre part, cuillerent et assemblerent grant ost et grant poer, chescune encountre altre, en les parties de Leycestre et en les parties de Bedeford. Meis qei par my lercevesqe Symond et ascuns autres evesqes et plousours autres grantz de la terre, forme dacord fu faite, et la partie le roi se humilia au roigne a respondre en parlement, et a drescer lerrour meu entre eux, par quei sur cel debat comence, et abesse pur eschuire greindre peril qe la terre ne livereit, et qe le roi seroit tenu pur seignur. Et pur ceo qe ascunes persones de Loundres furent venuz en la compaignie le dit sire Henry de Lancastre come encountre le roi. Meis qe la querele le counte fust dreiture, cestassavoire qil viveroit del soen pur maintenire sa terre, sil

(fo. 263v)

Ragman with the seals of homage done to the noble king Edward, grandfather of the present king, and to his heirs were returned to the said sir David, son and heir of the said sir Robert Bruce. And thus the Scots were fully released for ever from the lordship and from any sort of service due by right to the king of England and to his heirs. At this time the queen, mother of the new king, and sir Roger Mortimer usurped royal power and the treasure of the realm and they held the king under their subjection to such an extent that sir Henry, earl of Lancaster, who by common assent of the realm at the king's coronation was made his chief guardian, could not come near to him to advise him or protect him. For this reason the earl taking his own counsel and that of some lords of the realm and with the advice of master Simon Meopham, who was then archbishop of Canterbury, and other bishops, called upon the [queen's] side to put right the failure, so that the king might live as king, of his own, without making extortionate prises which impoverished his people. For this reason parliament was summoned at Salisbury, but no parliament was held because the parties nearly came to blows on Salisbury plain; but this was prevented on the advice of certain lords and parliament was then summoned for Candlemas [2 February].

In 1329 at the feast of St Hilary [13 January], the king on one side, through the counsel of his mother and of Mortimer, and the said sir Henry, earl of Lancaster, on the other side, collected and assembled a great army and great forces each against the other in the regions of Leicester and Bedford, but through archbishop Simon and certain other bishops and a number of lords of the land a form of agreement was made. The king's side humbled themselves to the queen, agreeing to answer in parliament and to make amends for the offences committed between them, on account of this dispute begun and now ended, and in order to prevent the country being delivered into greater danger, and so that the king would be held as lord. Because of this [dispute] some Londoners had come into the company of the said sir Henry Lancaster, as if to oppose the king, except that the cause of the earl was just, that is to say that he [the king] should live of his own to maintain his land if he

(fo. 264)

fust guerroie par my altres terres. Tost apres cel temps furent justice [*sic*] mandez de par le roi a la Gihale de Loundres come en aide del maire des viscountes et des aldermans, sanz blemure la fraunchise, et de justiser les meffesanz, et chastier les fous. En cel temps le roi ove simple compaignie des gentz passa outra mier au roi de Fraunce, pur son homage faire pur la terre de Gasgoigne, cestassavoire le venderdy en la feste de seint Austin. Meisme cel an le dimanche prochein devant la feste de seint Piere in cathedra, qe adonqe fust par une joedy, fust dame Phillipe roigne Dengleterre coroune a Westminstre ove grant joie et od grant honure. Et en le primere symaigne de quaresme le roi tint son parlement a Wyncestre, et la fu monsire Esmon de Wodestok counte de Kente attache, le mardy lendemain de seint Gregoire, le quel counte fu ficz du roi et uncle de cestui roi, et si estut il de hors la porte du chastel de Wyncestre a hure (de: *interlined*) prime qil fust jugge tanqe a vespre, qe nule alme ne lui voleit decoler pur pite. Meis qun ribaud de la mareschaucie le roi fust comande de lui decoler, cestassaver en la ville de seint Cuthbert, et en meisme le jour qe le dit counte de Kent fust attache et decole, come avant est dist, le counte de Nichole et autres graunz furent attachez, les queux furent lessez amayn prise. Et par cel encheson le seignur de Wake noble chivaler et loial od plusours autres nobles du roialme passerent la meer, et la se tindrent pur perils qe les poeient avenir de lour enemis.

Lan Mille CCCXXX sire Edward ficz de cestui roi Edward fu nee a Wodestok la xvij kalend de Juil qe fu le venderdy devant la feste de seint Butolf qe adonqe fu par une dymanche. En cel temps ala xvme de seint Michel le roi tint parlement a Notingham, et entendist et aperceust bien en moltz des maneres qil avoit fou counseil, et qil et son roialme furent en point destre perdues traiterousement, et son poeple destruit, par qei il prist cest affaire grossement au coer, et le venderdy a nuyt

(fo. 264)

was [not] at war in other lands. Soon after this time justices were sent by the king to the Guildhall of London to aid the mayor and sheriffs and aldermen, without prejudice to the franchise, and to do justice to malefactors and to punish fools. At this time, that is to say Friday, the feast of St Austin [26 May], the king with a small company of men crossed the sea to the king of France to do his homage for the land of Gascony. In the same year, on Sunday next before the feast of St Peter in Cathedra [18 February], which then was on a Thursday, lady Philippa, queen of England, was crowned at Westminster with great joy and great honour. And in the first week of Lent the king held his parliament at Winchester, and there sir Edmund of Woodstock, earl of Kent, was brought to trial on Tuesday the day after St Gregory [13 March]. This earl was son of the [late] king and uncle of this king. And so, because out of pity no one wanted to behead him, he stood outside the door of Winchester castle from the hour of prime, when he was sentenced, until vespers, when a menial retainer of the king's marshalsea was ordered to behead him, that is to say on the eve of St Cuthbert [19 March]. And on the same day as the said earl of Kent was tried and beheaded, as mentioned above, the earl of Lincoln and other lords were brought to trial. They were permitted to give sureties for their appearance in court. And for this reason the lord of Wake, a noble and loyal knight, with several other nobles of the realm crossed the sea and stayed there because of the dangers which might befall them from their enemies.

In 1330 lord Edward, son of this king Edward, was born at Woodstock on the seventeenth day before the kalends of July, which was the Friday before the feast of St Botolf [15 June], which was then on a Sunday. At this time, on the quinzaine of Michaelmas [13 October], the king held parliament at Nottingham and heard and clearly perceived many ways in which he had had foolish counsel and that he and his realm were on the point of being lost by treachery and his people destroyed. For this reason he took this affair greatly to heart and on the Friday night,

(fo. 264v)

lendemain de seint Luk il fist arrestre dedeinz le chastel de Notyngham privement ascunes persones, et les mist en sauve garde, et maunda trois persones a la Tour de Loundres le samady en la veille des apostres seint Symond et seint Jude, cestassaver sire Roger de Mortumer, sire Geffrey de Mortumer son ficz, sire Symond de Bereford, le quel sire Roger avoit acroche a lui roial poer et grant tresor et avoit empense a defaire le roi. (et son: *deleted in red ink*) Et le dit sire Geffrey se fist appeller meismes roi de folie. En cel temps le roi manda apres les graunz, qi furent alloignes hors de cest terre pur doute qils avoient del engin de felouns qi furent pres du roi et son conseil qils ne furent maubaillez pur lour querele come fust le dit counte de Kent par faux compassement des felouns, et qe les aloisnez venissent a lour terres en pees, et pur estre en parlement a drescer les errours de la terre, et abatre le venim de les faux compassanz qi fust adonqes en haute monte. Le lundy lendemain de seint Katerine le roi tint son parlement a Westminstre, le joedy apres, cestassaver en le veille de seint Andreu, fu le dit sire Roger de Mortumer counte de la Marche traine, et pendu a Loundres, et son corps pendist par commandement le roi deux jours et deux nuytz. Et adonqe fu le corps livere de la grace le roi a les freres menours de Loundres le samadie au seir, et fust illueqe enterre le dymanche ensuant. En cel parlement par commun conseil du roialme le roi seisist en sa main totes les terres qe dame Isabel sa mere avoit, et la fust graunte davoire chescune an du roi, pur son hostel tenire et garder, trois mille livres dargent apaier a quatre termes del an, a tote sa vie. Et le dit sire Symond de Bereford fu a cel parlement trayne et pendu a Loundres a la feste de seint Lucye.

Lan Mille CCCXXXI le jeody en la semaigne de Pasqes, le roi simplement passa la mere vers le roi de Fraunce pur son homage faire pur la terre de Gascoigne, et il fust illueqe honurablement resceu de touz les grantz de la terre. Et quant ils avoient fait son homage, et il revint hastivent dedeinz les xv jours apres, et cria

(fo. 264v)

the day after St Luke [19 October], he had certain men secretly arrested within Nottingham Castle and put them into custody and sent three men to the Tower of London on Saturday the eve of the Apostles Saints Simon and Judas [27 October], that is to say sir Roger Mortimer, sir Geoffrey Mortimer his son, [and] sir Simon Bereford. This sir Roger had usurped royal power and great treasure and had thought to overthrow the king, and the said sir Geoffrey through madness even called himself king. At this time the king sent for the lords who were in exile from this land through fear that they had of the schemes of the evil men who were near the king and his council, in case they should be severely dealt with for their action as the said earl of Kent had been by the deceitful conspiracy of the evil men. He [the king] ordered that those who had gone away should return to their lands in peace and be in parliament to put right the misgovernment of the land and to counteract the poison of the false conspirators which was then at its most potent. On Monday the day after St Katharine [26 November], the king held his parliament at Westminster. On the Thursday after, that is to say on the eve of St Andrew [29 November], the said sir Roger Mortimer, earl of March, was drawn and hanged at London and his body hanged by order of the king for two days and two nights. And then the body was handed over by the king's grace to the Franciscans of London on Saturday evening and it was buried there on the Sunday following. In this parliament by common counsel of the realm the king took into his hands all the lands which lady Isabella his mother had, and 3,000 pounds of silver were granted to her to have each year from the king in order to maintain and keep up her household, to be paid quarterly for all her life. And the said sir Simon Bereford was drawn and hanged at this parliament at London on the feast of St Lucy [13 December].

In 1331 on Thursday in Easter week [4 April] the king crossed the sea with a small company to the king of France to pay his homage for the land of Gascony and there he was honourably received by all the lords of the land. And when he had paid his homage, he came back swiftly within the following fortnight and proclaimed

(fo. 265)

solempne tournement a Derteford. Et puis en cel temps apres,
le lundy, cestassaver le tierce jour apres la feste de seint Matheu,
furent solempnes joustes en Chepe entre la croice et Sopereslane,
et furent faites barures dune part et dautre de bone meryn, et fu
graunt burdiz fait en haut en travers le rue, pur la roigne et
autres nobles dames pur veer la jouste, qe xiij chivalers avoient
pris encountre touz autres chivalers qi voleient venire pur
joustere, et durra la jouste par trois jours. En cel joust avint
une tiele aventure dount le poeple estoit molt effraie, quar si
come les chivalers mieutz jousteront apres manger le primer
jour, le hurdiz en haut qe fu faite de gros merine, la oue la
dame Philippe la roigne, et Alianore la soer le roi, et autres
grauntz dames de la terre, chivalers qi en lour compaignie
esturent pur veere jouste, cheit jus a terre. Et la roigne et autres
qi illueqes furent cheierent, issint qe dames et chivalers plusours
furent blessez, auxi bien de ceux qi furent esteantz par avale,
come de ceux qi furent par amont, meis nul ne fust peri, ne la
roigne ne la soer le roi ne furent en ceo cas blescez, come dieu
la voleit, mes qe le corinal la roigne cheist de sa teste et fust
debruse. La quele sodeine aventure fust par my la defaute des
carpenters. Et le roi de sa franche volente et graciouse grace et
par my la priere la dame la roigne pardona le trespas, et fist
crier pees par tut, et amour, et qe nul deveroit de rien estre
abaie ne affraie. Et le roi comanda la roigne en la meson dun
citein de la citee Nichol de Farndoun en Wodestret monter son
palefray en hast et chivaucher sus et jus el renk ove bele
semblaunt, a conforter le poeple, et le hurdiz, qe si sodoignement
cheist, fust reparaille de nuyt et fet assetz fort, issint qe
lendemain feu le jeu contenu noblement.

   Lan Mille CCCXXXII ala goule daugst sire Edward de
Baillolf, monsire Henry de Beaumond, le counte Dathels, le
counte de Anegos, sire Fouk[35] ficz Warin, sire Richard Talebot,
le Baroun de Stafford, et monsire Thomas Ughtred ove grant
ost et ove grant poer des Engleis vindrent par miere en les
parties

---

[35] *Margin*: Kynkehorn.

(fo. 265)

a grand tournament at Dartford. And after this time, on Monday, that is to say the third day after the feast of St Matthew [23 September], there were formal jousts in Cheapside between the Cross and Soper's Lane and on both sides barriers were made of good timber, and a great beam was put up above across the road for the queen and other noble ladies to see the joust that thirteen knights had undertaken against all other knights who wanted to come to joust; and the joust lasted for three days. In this joust an accident happened which greatly alarmed the people, for, as the knights jousted again after dinner on the first day, the upper staging, which was made of great timber, where the lady Philippa the queen, and Eleanor, the sister of the king, and other great ladies of the land, and the knights who were in their company were placed to see the joust, fell to the ground. The queen and the others who were there fell down, with the result that several ladies and knights were wounded, both those who had been above and those who were below, but no one was killed, nor were the queen or the king's sister injured in this affair, as God willed, except that the queen's coronet fell from her head and was broken. This sudden accident was due to the fault of the carpenters. The king of his free will and gracious mercy and through the prayers of the lady the queen pardoned the fault, and had peace and love proclaimed everywhere, and [proclaimed also] that no one should be in any way scared or afraid. And the king ordered the queen, who was in the house of a citizen of the city, Nicholas Farndon, in Wood Street, to mount her palfrey quickly and to ride up and down the lines with a good countenance to reassure the people. The staging which fell so suddenly was repaired at night and was made strong enough so that the next day the game was continued in a noble manner.

In 1332 on 1st August sir Edward Balliol, sir Henry Beaumont, the earl of Atholl, the earl of Angus, sir Fulk Fitz Warin, Richard Talbot, the baron of Stafford, and sir Thomas Ughtred with a great army and with a great force of Englishmen came by sea to

(fo. 265v)

Descoce, pur chalenger lour terres qe a eux furent de droit, queles terres furent liverez et donez as plusours grauntz seignurs Descoce sanz lour assent et volente. Et pur ceo qe le roi Edward ne voleit enfreindre ne destourber la pees taille entre lui et ceux Descoce, come avant est dite, il ne les voleit suffrire passer par my son roialme en la dite terre Descoce. Et pur ceo ils pristrent lou [sic] veage par eawe, come de sus est dite, dount en le viij^{me} ide daugst, cestassaver en la feste des seintz Sixti et Felicissimi, ils pristrent terre a Kyncorne en la counte de Fif. Et les Escoz a la mountance de x mille gaitauntz les Engleis pur prendre terre, et vindrent sur eux bataillez, et les archers Dengleterre et petit petaille, qavoient pris terre devant qe les gentz darmes poeient issire de lour niefs, assemblerent a les Escoce. Et tant firent qe les Escoz furent debotez, et furent occis bien a ix centz, et le remenant se mistrent a la fuite. Lendemain les gentz Dengleterre se mistrent vers labbeie de Dunfermelyn, ou ils troverent des vitailles a grant foison, et la les Engleis entendirent qe touz les grantz Descoz, od tout lour poer des gentz darmes et de pedaille, estoient apparaillez de venire sur eux (eux: *repeated, and deleted in red*) a la bataille, et furent venuz en une lieu appellez Gaskymore. Et ceo fust auxi come en la veille de seint Laurence, et ascuns de noz gentz furent grantment descounfortez pur la petit quantite des gentz, qar ils navoient en tote manere de gent qe ij mille et v^c, et les Escoce estoient a esmez xl mille. Et noz gentz demurerent tout le jour sur une rivere veaunt lour enemis. Et quant il estoit anuytez les Engleis passerent la rivere a une geye molt quorement, qe sire Alisaundre de Moubray cognust. Tant travaillerent il tote la nuyte qils estoient mountez tote la mountaigne oue les Escoce furent allogez a senestre, et purpristrent la grande more. Et quant il estoit cler jour lors sentrevirent lun ost lautre ost. Et les Escoz se merveillerent coment les Engleis avoient issint purpris la more, et maintenant crierent as armes, et les parties sassemblerent coraiousement

(fo. 265v)

Scotland to claim back the lands which were theirs by right, which lands without their assent or agreement had been handed over and given to several great lords of Scotland. And because king Edward did not wish to infringe or disturb the peace arranged between him and those of Scotland, as mentioned before, he would not allow them to cross through his realm into the said land of Scotland. Because of that they made their way by sea, as is related above, so that on the eighth day before the ides of August, that is to say on the feast of the Saints Sixtus and Felicissimus [6 August], they landed at Kinghorn in the county of Fife. And the Scots to the number of 10,000 were keeping watch for the English to land and approached them in battle array. The English archers and the small force of footmen, who landed before the men at arms could disembark from their ships, assembled against the Scots, and did so much that the Scots were repulsed and at least 900 were killed and the rest put to flight. The next day the English took themselves towards Dunfermline abbey where they found provisions in great abundance; and there the English heard that all the lords of Scotland with all their force of men at arms and of footsoldiers were ready to join battle with them and had come to a place called Gaskymore. And this was also on the eve of St Laurence [9 August], and some of our people were greatly dejected by the small number of their forces for they had in all manner of men only 2,500 and the Scots were estimated at 40,000. Our forces remained all day on a river watching their enemies. And when night had fallen the English crossed the river very quietly by a ford known to sir Alexander Mowbray. They laboured so much during the night that they had ascended the entire mountain where the Scots were positioned on the left, and took over the great moor. And when it was daylight there the two armies saw each other, and the Scots marvelled at the manner in which the English had thus taken over the moor. Now they cried to arms and the sides came together with spirit

(fo. 266)

sauve xl hommes darmes Dalemaine, qestoient venuz en aide des Engleis. Et tant firent les Engleis al aide de dieu qe la graunte multitude des Escoz estoit descounfiz et mortz et mis a la fuite. Et morurent a la bataille saunz menceynge dire del ost Descoz monsire Donald de Mar, le counte de Meneth, le counte Dathels, Descoz, le joefne, le counte de Murref, monsire Robert de Bruis counte de Karrik, monsire Neel de Bruis, monsire Alisaundre de Bruis, xij banerez, viij^{xx} chivalers, ij mille hommes darmes, et xiij mille et iij^c de pedaille. Et des Engleis morurent a la bataille monsire Johan Burdoun, monsire Reynaud de la Beche, et bien a xxxiij gentils hommes, nul archer ne nul homme a pee. Et ala nuyt al passage de la rivere (estoit neiez monsire Roger de Swinardestoun le fiz et)^{36} durra la bataille del solail levant tanqe a houre de tiers. Ceste descounfeture fu le mesqerdy prochein apres la feste de seint Laurenz. Lendemain les Engleis se remuerent vers la ville de seint Johan, et la pristrent sanz defense, et troverent illueqe assetz de vitailles, et se reposerent et afforcerent la ville de large fosse, et de peel, entendant qils en averoient mestre, et issint avoient ils hastivement, quar le counte Patrik et Archebaud Douglas amenerent devant la ville de tote manere de gent bien a xl mille. Et manderent a Berewyk apres Johan Crabbe qil vensit hastivement et sanz delay par mere od tot la navie et od tote la gente qil purreit assembler, et qil entroit leawe de Gye [sic], et qil deveroit ardre les nefs des Engleis sodeignement, et qil vensist a la ville de seint Johan a meintenire la siege devers leawe, sur quel maundement le dit Johan fist apparailler dis nefs de Flaundres, et mist leinz tut lestor qe li estoit bosoigne pur guerre, et des mellours in venceux de Berewyk et du paiis, et vint sodeynement sur les nefs des Engleis desgarniz, et al primer chief il trova la barge Beaumound, et la prist et occist tote la gent qe leinz fust, et pensa defere tiele mestrie des altres, meis il faillist, qar le petit ost des Engleis qestoient dedeinz lour niefs les porterent si bien qe les Escoz estoient desconfiz

---

^{36} Bodleian Library MS Lyell 17, fo. 120v.

(fo. 266)

except for forty German men at arms who had come to the aid of the English. And with the help of God the English did so much that the great multitude of Scots was defeated and killed and put to flight. There died in the battle, without a word of a lie, of the Scottish army, sir Donald of Mar, the earl of Menteith, the Scottish earl of Atholl, the younger, the earl of Moray, sir Robert Bruce, earl of Carrick, sir Neil Bruce, sir Alexander Bruce, twelve bannerets, 160 knights, 2,000 men at arms, and 13,300 footmen. And among the English there died in the battle sir John Burdon, sir Reynold de la Beche, and a good thirty-three noble men, [but] no archer nor any footman; and in the night at the crossing of the river (sir Roger Swinnerton, the younger, was drowned). The battle lasted from sunrise until the hour of tierce. This defeat was on the Wednesday next after the feast of St Laurence [12 August]. The next day the English moved off towards the town of Perth and took it without opposition and found a great quantity of provisions there. They rested, and fortified the town with a wide ditch and a peel, realising that they would have need of this, and indeed they did very soon for the earl Patrick and Archibald Douglas brought up to the town a good 40,000 of all manner of men. And they sent to Berwick for John Crabbe (and told him) to come by sea quickly and without delay with all the navy and with all the men whom he could assemble, and to enter the River Tay and rapidly to burn the ships of the English and to come to the town of Perth to maintain the siege on the water side. On this command the said John had ten Flemish ships made ready and put in them all the stores which he needed for war, and the best to be found in Berwick and the countryside. And he came suddenly on the unarmed English ships, and in the leading position he found the Beaumont barge and captured it and killed all the people who were in it, and he thought to have similar mastery over the others, but he failed, for the little army of the English who were in their ships bore themselves so well that the Scots were defeated

(fo. 266v)

en mier, et tote la greignure partie occis et noiez, et totes lour
niefs estoient arses et la barge ensement, et totes les nefs des
Engleis et tot lour gent sauvez par la vertue de dieu, fors ceux
qestoient primerement occis en la barge Beaumond. Et a grante
peine eschapa Johan Crabbe par terre et revint a Berwyk molt
dolerousement. Ceste aventure fu le jour de seint Barthelmeu.
Quant le counte Patrik et Erchebaud Douglas et altres qi
maintendrent la siege savoient ceste novele, ils se remuerent
dillueqe, et sen alerent saunz plus seger ou damager les Engleis,
od grant ost et od grant poer en le paiis de Galeway, qest al
seignur le Baillol, et la mistrent en feu et en flaum, et enchacerent
les gentz du paiis, et pristrent et emporterent quantqe ils poeient
trover. Meis quant sire Edward oierent cest novele hastiment
passerent la mere Descoce, pur les encountrer et rendre bataille
a eux, mes avant lour passage ils corounerent le dit sire[37]
Edward de Baillol roi Descoce a Skone. Denapres quant les
Escoz savoient la venue des Engleis qi noblement vindrent
encontre eux arraiez pur doner bataille a eux, et ils se mistrent
ala feute et noseient attendre. Puis le dit monsire Edward de
Baillol ove sez gentz qil avoit sen ala a Rokesburgh et la demura
une piece. Le counte Patrik, et Archebaud Douglas, et autres
grantz Descoce, qi furent demurez en vie, maunderent a sire
Edward de Baillol, qi adonqe fu fait roi Descoz par my le poer
des Engleis come devant est (dit: *interlined*), qil lor donast
trewes tanqe ala Chaundeleure, qe le roi poeit pleinement
parlement tenir en bien pees pur acordre, et unire, et estre une
gent. Le roi Descoce, qi ne pensa de nul tresoun, les graunta, et
remua sa gent, et les felouns Descoce al noumbre de dis mille
vindrent lendemain de seint Martin bien armes, et comencerent
tiwer quantqe ils poeient happer de la partie le roi qi furent
desarmez, et le roi meismes a grante peine sen fuist oue
autrement il eust este trahi. Mes sire Thomas Ughtred, qi
adonqe estoit noble chivaler et vaillant, od dis hommes darmes
tauntsoulement

---

[37] *Margin*: hic coronatur E. Baillof.

(fo. 266v)

at sea, and all the greater part killed and drowned, and all their
ships were burned and the barge similarly, and all the English
ships and all their men were saved by the virtue of God except
those who were first killed in the Beaumont barge. With great
difficulty John Crabbe escaped by land and came back to
Berwick with great sorrow. This event was on St Bartholomew's day [24 August]. When the earl Patrick and Archibald
Douglas and the others who were maintaining the siege heard
this news they moved away from there and, without prolonging
the siege or damaging the English, went away with a great
army and great force into the country of Galloway, which
belonged to the lord Balliol, and put it to fire and flame, and
drove the people from the country and took and carried off
everything they could find. But when sir Edward heard this
news he quickly crossed the Scottish sea to meet and give battle
to them. But before they crossed they crowned the said sir
Edward Balliol king of Scotland at Scone. Afterwards, when
the Scots learnt of the coming of the English who came against
them honourably arrayed to give battle, they fled and dared
not wait. Then the said sir Edward Balliol, with the men he
had with him, went to Roxburgh and stayed there a while.
The earl Patrick and Archibald Douglas and other Scottish
lords who were still alive sent to ask sir Edward Balliol, who
then had been made king of Scotland through the English
might as previously mentioned, that he should grant them
truces until Candlemas [2 February], so that the king might
hold a full parliament in good peace, in order to make accord
and to unite them together into one people. The king of
Scotland, who did not suspect treason, granted them this and
sent away his forces, and the evil men of Scotland to the
number of 10,000 came well armed the day after St Martin [13
or 11 November], and began to kill all whom they could catch
of the king's side who were unarmed; and the king himself
with great difficulty fled or otherwise he would have been
betrayed. But sir Thomas Ughtred who was a noble and valiant
knight with only ten men at arms

(fo. 267)

combatirent fortiblement ove les Escoz lour enemis, et les
rechacerent de la pount, et grante partie de eux furent occis et
neiez, et le remenant se mist a la feuite. Et tost vindrent aide et
socours a sire Edward de Baillol et a ses gentz, et hastivement
ensiwerent les fuauntz, et oscirent quantqe ils poeient atteindre
et trover, et illueqe fu pris Andreu de Moret et altres, meis
Johan Crabbe od grante peine eschapa, et dolerousement sen
fuist a Berewyk et la se tint. Denapres sire Edward de Baillol
entra la terre Descoz od les grantz seignurs Dengleterre et od
lour gentz, le samady en la semaine de quaresme, et
chivaucherent en plusours lieus de la terre, et firent grantz
maux a lour enemis. Et les sires de Mountagu, de Percy, de
Neville le ficz, le counte de Lancastre, et le counte Darundelle
pristrent une peel, en le quel ils troverent monsire Robert de
Colville et x hommes darmes, plusours femmes du paiis,
dames, et autres, et demene gent une partie, et grant fuson de
vitailles, et tut amenerent il ovesqe eux, et destruerent le peel.
Puis sen alerent a Berewyk pur asseger la ville par terre et par
eawe, et ficherent lour pavillons, et fesoient plusours assautz a
la ville, meis ceux dedeinz se defenderent vigerousement. Et
tant come la siege se durra les avantditz nobles Dengleterre od
moltz des gentz darmes et od grandesme ost passerent avant en
la terre Descoz, pur encountrer lour enemis, meis ils ne
troverent nul encountre, par quei ils revendrent joiousement a
Berewyk, et fesoient einsi lour parlance ove les juvencels de la
dite ville, qe la ville deust aver este rendu a eux come al oeps le
roi Dengleterre, et noun pas al oeps sire Edward de Baillol. Et
quant la communalte de Berewyk avoit aperceu coment les
juvencels de la dite ville voleient avere rendu la ville au roi
Dengleterre et a sire Edward de Baillol sanz lour congie et lour
assent, ils estoient grandement grevez et corucez, et hastivement
mounterent les murs de la dite ville et noblement la defenderent
encountre les Engleis. Et quant les Engleis virent qe la
communalte de la ville ne voleint assentir en nul manere au roi
Dengleterre, ne a sire Edward le

(fo. 267)

fought vigorously against their Scottish enemies, and drove them back from the bridge and a great part of them were killed and drowned and the rest fled. And soon after aid and help came to sir Edward Balliol and to his forces and they quickly followed the fleeing men and killed whomever they could capture and discover; and Andrew Moray and others were taken there, but John Crabbe escaped with great difficulty and fled with much sorrow to Berwick and stayed there. After this sir Edward Balliol entered Scotland with the great English lords and their forces on Saturday in the week of Lent [20 February] and raided several places in the land and did great damage to their enemies. And the lords Montagu, Percy, Neville the younger, the earl of Lancaster, and the earl of Arundel took possession of a peel in which they found sir Robert Colville and ten men at arms, a number of local women, ladies and others, and some of their own people and great plenty of provisions, and took everyone away with them and destroyed the peel. Then they went to Berwick to besiege the town by land and by sea and set up their tents and made several assaults on the town, but those within defended themselves vigorously. And while the siege lasted the aforesaid English nobles with many men at arms and with a very large army crossed into Scotland to meet their enemies, but they met no one, on account of which they returned happily to Berwick and spoke thus with the young men of the said town, saying that the town ought to be given over to them to the use of the king of England and not to the use of sir Edward Balliol. When the commonalty of Berwick had perceived how the young men of the said town wanted to give the town to the king of England and to sir Edward Balliol without their leave and assent, they were greatly aggrieved and angered and quickly mounted the walls of the said town and honourably defended it against the English. And when the English saw the commonalty of the town did not wish to accommodate themselves in any way to the king of England nor to sir Edward Balliol

(fo. 267v)

Baillof, ils lesserent lour sege et se remuerent dillueqe et vindrent en Engleterre. En cel temps le roi tint son parlement a Everwyk, a queu parlement ils y vindrent monsire Henry de Beaumond, le counte Dathels, le counte Dangos, sire Richard Talebot, sire Fouk ficz Warin, le Baron de Stafford, sire Thomas Wghtred et plusours autres, pur treter et ordener dascuns busoignes et esploites touchantz les roialmes Dengleterre et Descoz. Et tant come ils feurent einsi pur parlementre, les gentz Descoz, qi touz jours furent faux et compassantz de mal, vindrent a sire Edward de Baillof et autrefoiz li prierent de enduces, issint qe le dit sire Edward les graunta par conseil et assent dascuns desloiaux qi furent adonqe pred lui, par quei les Escoz vindrent apres sodeinement armes od grant poer, cestassaver sire Archebald Douglas, dustre del ost Descoce, et seneschal de la terre, le counte Patryk, et plusours autres, et firent grant mal au dit sire Edward de Baillol, oscirent ses gentz et les robberent, et lour biens emporterent, meis avint issint al aide de dieu qe plusours grantz seignurs de la partie Descoz furent illuqe occis, cestassaver sire Johan de Moubray Descoz, sire Walter Comyn, sire William de la Beche, sire Johan Talebot, et plusours autres, et le roi Descoce avoit la victorie.

Lan Mille CCCXXXIII plusours grauntz seignurs Dengleterre revindrent a Berewyk, et autrefoicz assegerent la ville et ne voleient departire dillueqe tanqe la ville fu rendu a lour volunte. Les Escoce avoient dedeinz la ville grant ost et fort, et noblement la defenderent encountre eux, meis ils noseient isser hors pur doner bataille a les Engleis, qils avoient assege, par quei le dite Archebaud Douglas et autres grauntz Descoz al noumbre de trois mille entrerent les parties de Northumbre et en Gisland prede la cite de Cardoille, et mistrent en feu et en flaume les terres qe furent a monsire Randolf de Dacre, xv liwes en longure et vj liwes en leoure, et se retournerent od petite praie. En meisme cel temps monsire Antoyne de Lucy et William de Loghmaban entrerent la terre

(fo. 267v)

they raised their siege and moved from there and came into England. At this time the king held his parliament at York, to which parliament there came sir Henry Beaumont, the earl of Atholl, the earl of Angus, sir Richard Talbot, sir Fulk Fitz Warin, the baron of Stafford, sir Thomas Ughtred and several others to treat and make arrangements about certain tasks and undertakings touching the realms of England and Scotland. And while they were there in this manner to confer, the people of Scotland, who were always false and conspiring evil, came to sir Edward Balliol and again begged him for a truce, so that the said sir Edward granted it to them with the advice and assent of certain disloyal men who were then with him. Afterwards, because of this the Scots suddenly came, armed with great force, that is to say Archibald Douglas, leader of the Scottish army and steward of the land, the earl Patrick and several others, and they did great harm to the said sir Edward Balliol, killed his people and robbed them and carried away their goods; but it so happened that, by God's help, several great Scottish lords were killed there, that is to say sir John Mowbray of Scotland, sir Walter Comyn, sir William de la Beche, sir John Talbot and several others, and the king of Scots won the day.

In 1333 several great English lords came again to Berwick and once more besieged the town and did not want to leave there until the town was given to their will. The Scots had a great and strong force within the town and they defended it nobly against them [the English], but they dared not sally forth to give battle to the English who had besieged them. For this reason the said Archibald Douglas and other Scottish lords to the number of 3,000 entered Northumberland and Gilsland near the city of Carlisle and put to fire and flame the lands fifteen leagues long and six leagues wide which belonged to sir Randolph Dacre, and returned with little booty. At the same time sir Anthony Lucy and William of Lochmaben crossed into

(fo. 268)

Descoce od viij^c hommes, et chivaucherent la nuyte xx lieux. Et donqe retournerent ils, et le jeody en la feste del Annunciacion de Notre Dame matin comencerent il de ardre et de tiwire quant qe fu devant eux, et pristrent berbiz et autres grosses bestes a grant foison. Et a lour retourner William Douglas, qi fu gardein del dit peel de Loughmaban, et autres od grant nombre de gentz a hure de noune assaillerent le dit monsire Antoyne de Lucy et sez gentz, et fu la medle grant, meis les Escoz furent descomfitz, et furent pris le dite William Douglas, William Barde, et bien cent autres prisoners,[38] et monsire Humfrey du Jardyn chivalers, William de Cardoille et plousours autres a la montance de viij^{xx} des vallantz hommes furent illueqes occis, et le dite monsire Antoyn naufre, et retournereit sauvent en lour marches od lour preie.

Lan Mille CCCXXXIIII[39] quant le roi Dengleterre avoit oi coment les Escoz avoient (faite: *in right margin*) arsours, robberies, et homicides de sa terre, en contre la forme du pees taille entre eux, il prist od li le counte de Garrenne, le counte de Warwyk, le counte de Nichole, le counte de Cornewaille, les seignurs de Wak, de Ros, de Moubray, de Clifford, de Crumbewelle, sire Fouk ficz Waryn, et monsire Johan de Roos, od grant multitude des gentz darmes, et de pedaille, et darchers, et dautres prestz et apparailles a la bataille, et entrerent les parties de Northumbre les desleaux meffesaunz et pariours les Escoz sez enemis et a combatre ove eux. Meis quant les Escoz savoient la venue le roi Dengleterre, ils sen fuirent en Escoce come cowartz qi nul bataille noseient. Meisme lan le xvij kalend de Juyn, le roi passa leawe prede Berewyk, et entra la terre Descoz, et le xv kalend de Juyn ceux qavoient assege la dite ville de Berewyk donerent fort assaut a lour enemis, meis ceux dedeinz se defendirent bien a lour poer. Meis avint issint a cel assaut qe moltz des maux avindrent auxi bien a les Engleis qi fesoient la sege, come a ceux qi furent dedeinz, pur la dite ville defendre. Meis

[38] Bodleian Library MS Lyell 17, fo. 121v, adds the name of Hunfrey de Boys here; see introduction p. 57.
[39] *Recte* XXXIII.

(fo. 268)

Scotland with 800 men and rode twenty leagues during the night. And then they returned and on Thursday the feast of the Annunciation of Our Lady [25 March 1333], in the morning, they began to burn and kill all before them, and they took sheep and other fat beasts in great plenty. At their return William Douglas who was keeper of the said peel of Lochmaben and others with a great number of men at the hour of none attacked the said sir Anthony Lucy and his men, and there was a great mêlée, but the Scots were defeated, and the said William Douglas, William Baird and a good 100 others were taken prisoner, and sir Humphrey Jardyn, knight, William Carlisle and many others to the number of 160 of the valiant men were killed there, and the said sir Anthony was wounded, and they returned safely to their borders with their booty.

In [1333] when the king of England heard how the Scots had committed arson, robbery and murder in his land despite the form of peace agreed between them, he took with him earl Warenne, the earl of Warwick, the earl of Lincoln, the earl of Cornwall, the lords Wake, Ros, Mowbray, Clifford, Cromwell, sir Fulk Fitz Warin, and sir John Roos with a great multitude of men at arms and footsoldiers and archers and others ready and equipped for battle and entered Northumberland, [to seek] the disloyal, the evildoers, and the associates of his Scottish enemies, and to do battle with them. But when the Scots learnt of the arrival of the king of England they fled into Scotland like cowards who did not dare do battle. In the same year, on the seventeenth day before the kalends of June [16 May], the king crossed the water near Berwick and entered Scotland, and on the fifteenth day before the kalends of June [18 May] those who had been besieging the said town of Berwick launched a strong attack against their enemies, but those within defended themselves with all their might. But it so happened in this attack that many evils befell both the English who conducted the siege and those who were inside defending the said town. But

(fo. 268v)

quant le roi et les gentz Dengleterre avoient entendu la malice
de ceux qi furent dedeinz la dite ville de Berewyk, ils
comanderent lour gentz de doner molt plus fort assaut qonqes
devant navoient faite, et ils ainsi firent par eawe et par terre, et
jetterent feu dedeinz la ville, et arderent eglises et mesons
plusours, et fesoient moltz des maux a lour enemis, par quei
les Escoz manderent au roi Dengleterre, et li prierent de trewes
tanqe al quart jour de Juyn, en promettantz de rendre ali la
ville, si aide ne lour vensist le plus tost de lour gentz demene,
le roi par conseil de sez gentz granta bonement la trewe, et
comanda sez gentz cesser de lour assaut, et qe nul Engleis ne
feist male ne grevance a ceux qi furent dedeinz la ville, par quei
ceux dedeinz la ville avoient repos de assaut faire, et se tindrent
en pees une piece. Meis tost apres ils vindrent encountre la dite
trewe come ceux qestoient faux et pleins de mencionges, quar
devant la fine de la dite trewe, ils se apparaillerent atrefoiz de
doner assaut a les Engleis, et a defendre la ville encountre eux,
par quei le roi Edward Dengleterre comanda sez gentz autrefoicz
apparailler engins et autre attilementz affaire assaut a la dite
ville, et hastivement la prendre a force. Et quant les Escoz
savoient ceste novele, ils se doterent durement perdre lour ville,
et estre confoundez, et destrutz, et altrefoicz manderent a
monsire Edward roi Dengleterre, et li prierent de trewe tanqe
a viij jours procheins ensiwauntz, sur tiele forme qe, sils
autrefoicz enfreindroient la dite trewe, ils perdroient la dite
ville arement, le roi Dengleterre qi molt estoit homme de pite
et de mercy, et autrefoicz les granta, et fist son serement qe sils
estoient altrefoiz fauses devers li qils naveroient ja merci de eux
pur raunson ne pur prier. Tost apres vindrent en Engleterre lx
mille des Escoz encountre la ville de Berewyk, et departirent
entre eux et les Engleis leawe de Twede, pur aver done bataille
a ceux qi assegerent

(fo. 268v)

when the king and the English had heard of the wickedness of those who were within the said town of Berwick they ordered their men to launch a much greater assault than they had previously done, and they did so by sea and by land and threw fire into the town and burned a number of churches and houses and did much harm to their enemies. For this reason the Scots sent to the king of England and begged him for a truce until 4 June, promising to give the town to him if help should not come to them immediately from their own people. The king with the advice of his men kindly granted the truce and ordered his forces to stop their assault and that no Englishman should harm or injure those who were in the town. Therefore those inside the town had a respite from the assault and they kept the peace a while, but soon after they broke the said truce like men who were false and full of lies, for before the end of the said truce they armed themselves again to attack the English and to defend the town against them. For this reason king Edward of England again ordered his men to prepare engines and other equipment to make an assault on the said town and to take it quickly by force. And when the Scots became aware of this they feared very much that they would lose their town and be beaten and destroyed and they again sent word to sir Edward king of England; they begged him for a truce for the eight days next following in such form that if they should break the said truce again they should lose the said town immediately. The king of England, who was very much a man of pity and mercy, again granted it them and took his oath that if they were again false towards him that they should not then have mercy for love or money. Soon after, 60,000 Scots came into England against the town of Berwick, leaving between them and the English the River Tweed, in order to give battle to those who besieged

(fo. 269)

la dite ville et remuere la dite sege sils poeient. Meis come dieu le voleit ils furent encountrez et rebotez, dount le roi Dengleterre pur lour grant desloialte, et pur ceo qils avoient enfreint lour jour de pees, ne voleient rendre a lui la dite ville de Berewyk come covenant fust, il fist pendre veauntz les Escoz le ficz monsire Alisandre de Setoun, le jour de seint Anaclete. Et quant ceo fu faite les Escoz fesoient assavoire au roi Dengleterre qils voleient venire combatre ov ly, en la veille de seint Margarete, et remuer la dite siege. Et quant le roi Edward Dengleterre savoit ceste novele il estoit joious et lee, et hastivement fist maundre et assembler touz les graunz Dengleterre qi furent illueqes ove lui venuz, pur ordener et conseiller coment ils poeient mieultz contreestere la malice de les Escoz lour enemis, et sauver ceux qi furent a la dite siege de Berewyk. Et issint conseillerent ils entre eux, qi parties des gentz le roi deust demurer od ceux qi assegerent la dite ville come en aide de eux, encountre lour enemis, sils sen eussent mester, et le remenant le roi deust retenir od li pur combatre encounte la grant multitude Descoce. Den apres en la dite veille de seinte Margarete, lan de grace avant dit, vint le grant ost Descoz, de quel le noumbre estoit iiij^{xx} mille, pres de la dite wille [sic] de Berewyk encountre lost le roi Dengleterre, et vindrent serement od lour ost bataillez en quatre batailles, et le roi Dengleterre et sez gentz vindrent encountre eux bataillez en meisme la manere. Meis les Escoz avoient si grant ost et si grant poer, qe quant les gentz Dengleterre avoient le vewe de eux, ils estoient grantement abaiz. Et ceo fu pur la reson qe lost Descoce lour enemis fust si grant et si fort encountre lost Dengleterre qe adonqe nestoit qe petist, meis le roi Edward (Edward: *repeated and deleted in red*) Dengleterre chivaucha par tut son ost, et conforta sez gentz bien et noblement, et les premist largement bone guerdoun, a y tiels qils se portassent bien encontre la grande multitude Descoce lour enemis,

(fo. 269)

the said town and to raise the said siege if they could. But as God willed it they were met and repulsed. Therefore the king of England, for their great disloyalty and because they had broken their day of peace and would not give him the said town of Berwick as the agreement was, had the son of sir Alexander Seton hanged in view of the Scots on the day of St Anacletus [12 July]. And when this was done the Scots made it known to the king of England that they would come to fight with him on the eve of St Margaret [19 July], and lift the said siege. And when the king of England heard this he was joyful and happy and quickly had all the English lords who had come there with him summoned and assembled, in order to plan and advise on how they could best oppose the wickedness of their Scottish enemies and save those who were at the said siege of Berwick. And so they decided among themselves that some of the king's forces should stay with those who besieged the said town as help for them against their enemies if they should have need of it, and the king should keep the rest with him to fight against the great multitude of Scots. After that, on the said eve of St Margaret [19 July], in the year of grace aforesaid, the great Scottish army which numbered 80,000 approached the said town of Berwick against the king of England's army and they came in close order, with their army drawn up in four battle lines, and the king of England and his people came against them drawn up in the same manner. But the Scots had so great an army and such a great force that when the English saw them they were very cast down. This was because the army of their Scottish enemies was so great and so strong compared with the English army which was then only small, but king Edward of England rode about everywhere among his army and encouraged his men well and nobly, and generously promised them good reward provided that they conducted themselves well against the great multitude of their Scottish enemies.[40]

---

[40] The short continuation of the French prose *Brut* appears to end about here; the account of Halidon Hill is peculiar to the Anonimalle narrative.

(fo. 269v)

si qe en la primere bataille des Escoz ili vindrent le (le: *repeated*) counte de Mouref et od li a baner monsire James Fryselle, monsire Symond Fryselle, monsire Walter Stiward, monsire Reynald Cleyme, monsire Patrik de Graham, monsire Johan Graunde, monsire James de Cardoille, monsire Patrik de Chartris, monsire Robert de Caldecotes, monsire Philippe Mildroun, monsire William Hardyn, monsire Thomas Cherpatrik, monsire Gilbert Wysman, monsire Adam Burdoun, monsire Johan de (de: *repeated*) Burgh, monsire James de Graveuasch, monsire Johan Grandels le ficz, monsire Robert Barde, et ovesqe eux vj^c hommes darmes, et xiiij mille CC de la commune, et xl bachilers. En la my garde le seneschalle Descoce, le counte de Meneth, sire James son uncle, sire William Douglas, sire Johan le ficz Johan de Galeway, sire David de Lindesey, sire Maucoloun Flemyng, sire William de Keth, sire David Kambel, sire James Stiward de Aldyngtoun, sire Johan de Burgh, sire Aleine Stiward, sire William de Aberconeweye, sire William Hirchyn, sire William Albertyn, sire William de Morref le ficz, sire Johan le ficz sire William, sire Adam de Murref de Layntoun, sire Johan de Shirestoun, et odvesqe eux vij^c hommes darmes, et xvij mille de la commune. En la terce bataille le counte de Roos, le counte de Shornlond, le counte de Straverne, sire Walter de Chilteleye, sire Johan Cambron, sire Gilbert de la Haye, sire David de Mar, sire Griffyn de la Harde, sire Johan Brounynge, et ovesqe eux ix^c hommes darmes, et xv mille de la commune, et xxx bachilers. En la quatre bataille sire Archebaud Douglas, (le: *interlined*) counte de Levenax, sire Alisaundre de Roos, seignur de Laverne, (le counte: *added in right margin*) de Fif, sire Johan Cambel qe se cleyme counte Dathels, sire Robert Loweder, ficz, sire William de Wippount, sire William de Hingestoun, sire Johan de Landels, sire Joce de Semperlowe, sire William Frisel, sire Johan de Lindeseye de Walpole, sire Alisaundre le Grey, sire Thomas de Bois, sire Roger le Mortumer,

(fo. 269v)

Thus in the first battle line of the Scots there came the earl of Moray, and with him under his banner sir James Fraser, sir Simon Fraser, sir Walter Stewart, sir Reginald Cheyne, sir Patrick Graham, sir John Grant, sir James Carlisle, sir Patrick Charteris, sir Robert Caldicott, sir Philip Meldrum, sir William Harden, sir Thomas Kirkpatrick, sir Gilbert Wiseman, sir Adam Burdon, sir John de Burgh, sir James of Garioch, sir John Grant [?] the son, sir Robert Baird, and with them 600 men at arms and 14,200 of the commonalty and forty bachelors. In the mid-guard [came] the Steward of Scotland, the earl of Menteith, sir James [Menteith] his uncle, sir William Douglas, sir John the son of John of Galloway, sir David Lindsay, sir Malcolm Fleming, sir William Keith, sir David Campbell, sir James Steward of 'Aldyngtoun', sir John de Burgh, sir Alan Steward, sir William Abernethy, sir William Erskine, sir William Abercorn [?Mure of Abercorn], sir William Murray the son, sir John the son of sir William, sir Adam Murray of 'Layntoun', sir John of 'Shirestoun', and with them 700 men at arms and 17,000 of the commonalty. In the third battle line [came] the earl of Ross, the earl of Sutherland, the earl of Strathearn, sir Walter Chisholm [?], sir John Cameron, sir Gilbert Hay, sir David of Mar, sir Cristin del Ard, sir John Browning, and with them 900 men at arms and 15,000 of the commonalty and thirty bachelors. In the fourth battle line [came] sir Archibald Douglas, the earl of Lennox, sir Alexander Ross, [the] lord of Lorn, the earl of Fife, sir John Campbell who calls himself earl of Atholl, sir Robert Lauder the son, sir William Vieuxpont, sir William of Whinkerstone, sir John Laundels, sir Joce of Lempitlaw, sir William Fraser, sir John Lindsay of Wauchope, sir Alexander Gray, sir Thomas Boyce, sir Roger Mortimer,

(fo. 270)

et ovesqe eux ix^c hommes darmes, et xviij mille de la commune, et iiij^{xx} bachelers, monsire Patrik de Dunbarre gardein du chastel de Berewyk, et od ly l hommes darmes, od la commune de la ville sanz nombre. Quant le counte de Mouref et les altres grantz Descoz avoient ainsi arraiez et batailles lour gentz en la manere susdite, le roi et les grantz Dengleterre arraierent et mistrent en eschele lour petites gentz al mieutz qils savoient et poient, et le roi Dengleterre conforta grantement sez gentz, et nomement les archers qi furent venuz en aide de li, et les premist bone guerdoun. Atant monsire Edward roi Dengleterre et ses gentz se mistrent avant hardiement el noum de Dieu vers lour enemis. Et les Escoz esturent en pees, et ne se voleient assembler au roi Dengleterre ne a sez gentz, et ceo fu par la resoun qils ne voleient remuer dillueqe tanqe leawe de Twede eust este pleinement montee de la meer, pur ceo qils adonqe bien quiderent qils dussent aver enchacez le roi Dengleterre et ses gentz en leawe de Twede oue en la mier pur les aver noie, meis, come Dieu le voleit, ils furent deceuz, qar les Engleis od lour petite poer des gentz se mistrent egrement et de bon coer encountre les Escoz lour enemis. Et le roi Dengleterre meismes fu le primer home qi se mist a la primere bataille Descoz, et les archers Dengleterre les desbaretta et greva, ainsi qils estoient en petite hure auxi come estuffez et envoegles, et tost perdirent lour contenance. Et les nobles Dengleterre se assemblerent a les autres escheles Descoz, et occirent illueqe tant de poer qe merveille y fust del veer et del penser. En quel bataille furent occis de la regioun Descoce viij contes, xiij barons, cestassaver les countes de Roos, de Mouref, de Straverne, de Southhirland, de Karryk, de Levenax, de Athels, et de Menteth, sire William Douglas, sire James Siward, sire James de Althill, sire James Fresil, sire Johan de Burgh, sire Robert de Keth, sire William de Wippont, sire William Burdoun, sire Adam Burdoun, sire Johan le ficz Johan de Galeway, sire William de Keth, sire William de

(fo. 270)

and with them 900 men at arms and 18,000 of the commonalty and eighty bachelors, sir Patrick Dunbar, keeper of the castle of Berwick, and with him fifty men at arms and the commonalty of the town without number. When the earl of Moray and the other Scottish lords had thus arrayed and drawn up their forces in the manner described above, the king and the English lords marshalled and put their small force into position as seemed best and most possible to them, and the king of England greatly encouraged his men and especially the archers who had come to his aid, and promised them good reward. Then sir Edward, king of England, and his forces advanced boldly in the name of God against their enemies. And the Scots stood quietly and did not wish to fight against the king of England and his forces and this was because they did not want to move from there until the River Tweed was at full flood tide, because they then well imagined that they might drive the king of England and his men into the River Tweed or into the sea to drown them. But by God's will they were mistaken, for the English with their little band of men vigorously and in good heart engaged their Scottish enemies. And the king of England himself was the first man who engaged the first battle line of the Scots, and the English archers destroyed and injured them so that they were in a short time as if choked and blinded, and soon they were thrown into confusion. And the English nobles attacked the other Scottish squadrons and killed there so many of the force that it was a marvel to see and contemplate. In this battle line, from the Scottish region were killed eight earls, thirteen barons, that is to say the earls of Ross, Moray, Strathearn, Sutherland, Carrick, Lennox, Atholl and Menteith, sir William Douglas, sir James Steward, sir James 'de Althill' [? James Stewart of 'Aldyngtoun'], sir James Fraser, sir John de Burgh, sir Robert Keith, sir William Vieuxpont, sir William Burdon, sir Adam Burdon, sir John the son of John of Galloway, sir William Keith, sir William

(fo. 270v)

Aberynthy et plusours (altres: *interlined*), dount le noumbre des gentz darmes qi illueqes furent trovez occis estoit xxx mille et plus, horspris autres valiantz gentz et pedaille. Quant plusours grantz seignurs Descoce virent coment les nobles de lour roialme furent einsi destruitz et maumenez par le roi Dengleterre et sez gentz, ils se mistrent a la fuite, et ascuns sen fuirent, et les noierent od grant dolour. Et le roi Dengleterre et Descoce pursiwerent les fuiantz coraiousement par terre, et occirent enfuant plus qe x mille, en cele purseute estoit monsire Johan de Neville occis, et xij autres de la commune Dengleterre. Quant ceo fu fait le roi Dengleterre returna vers Berewyk pur prendre la ville. Et les Escoz, qi dedeinz furent esteauntz sur les murs pur regarder la bataille avant dite, rendirent lendemain la dite ville de Berewyk au dite roi Dengleterre a sa volente, et le chastel ovesqe. Meisme cel an murust meistre Symond de Mepham ercevesqe de Caunterbury, a quel erceveschee fust eslu meistre Johan de Strayford adonqe evesqe de Wyncestre. Et fu mis en son lieu, meistre Adam de Hereford adonqes evesqe de Wyrcestre, qi avant fu evesqe de Hereford, et del evesche de Wircestre fu fet evesqe mestre Symond de Mountagu, frere a monsire William de Mountagu, qi puis estoit fait counte de Salesbury come vous orrez apres. Meisme cel an murust sire Lowiz de Beaumont evesqe de Duresme, et fust eslu danz Robert de Graystoun, moyne de la dite meisoun, et sacre de sire William de Meltoun ercevesqe Deverwyk, meis il fust ouste del erceveschee (erce: *deleted in red*) pur ceo qe le pape primes avoit donee le dite evesche a sire Richard de Bury, cestassavoir a la requeste le roi Dengleterre, et ceo fu par la reson qe le dite sire Richard fust prive et bene ame du roi, et longement (avoit: *interlined*) este en service le roi. Mesme cel an dame Isabel la fille le roi fu nee a Wodestok.

Lan Mille CCCXXXIII le xj kalend de Juyl monsire Edward de Baillol roi Descoce, en la presence des plusours grantz seignurs Dengleterre et Descoz, fist son homage au roi Dengleterre[41] pur le dit roialme Descoz, a aver et tenire au dite roi Dengleterre et a sez heirs a touz

---

[41] *Margin*: homage fait al roy dengleterre par le roy Descoce.

(fo. 270v)

Abernethy, and many others, of which the number of men at arms who were found killed there was 30,000 and more, quite apart from other valiant people and footmen. When several great lords of Scotland saw how the nobles of their realm were thus destroyed and wounded by the king of England and his people they took to flight and some fled away, and drowned in great sorrow. And the king[s] of England and of Scotland courageously pursued those fleeing by land and killed in flight more than 10,000. In this pursuit sir John Neville and twelve others of the commonalty of England were killed. When this was done the king of England returned towards Berwick to take the town. And the Scots who were within, being on the wall to see the battle described above, surrendered the said town of Berwick the next day to the will of the said king of England, and the castle with it. This same year master Simon Meopham archbishop of Canterbury died; to this archbishopric master John Stratford, then bishop of Winchester, was elected. And master Adam of Hereford was put in his place, and master Simon Montagu, brother of sir William Montagu, who was afterwards made earl of Salisbury as you will learn later, was made bishop of the bishopric of Worcester. This same year sir Lewis de Beaumont bishop of Durham died and dom Robert Graystanes, a monk of the said house, was elected and consecrated by sir William Melton archbishop of York, but he was removed from the bishopric because the pope had previously given the said bishopric to sir Richard Bury, that is to say at the request of the king of England. This was because the said sir Richard was a close friend and well loved by the king and had been long in the king's service. In this same year lady Isabella the king's daughter was born at Woodstock.

In 1333, on the eleventh day before the kalends of July [21 June], sir Edward Balliol, king of Scotland, in the presence of several great lords of England and Scotland paid his homage to the king of England for the said realm of Scotland, to have it and hold it from the said king of England and his heirs for

(fo. 271)

jours, endonant al avantdit roi Dengleterre et a sez heirs la ville de Berewyk ove le counte. Meisme cel an le quinte noun de Decembre murust le pape Johan le XXII a Avynoun, et le jour d[e] dimenche fust enterre en la graunde eglise prede le paleis, fait assaver qe meisme cel temps qe le dite sire Edward de Baillol fist son homage, le counte Patryk fist le soen homage a roi Dengleterre destre foial et loial a li et a sez heirs a touz jours, a tenire de li et de ses heirs ses terres, les queux il avoit el roialme Descoz, et estre ceo il premist au dite roi Dengleterre, de faire touz les grantz (Descoce: *interlined*) estre enclinantz et subitz a li, et a monsire Edward de Baillol qi estoit roi Descoz. Et pur ceste chose avant dite, le roi Dengleterre li dona grante somme davoire, cestassaver mille livres, pur redresser et reparaillere ses manoirs et ses villes, les queux gentz Dengleterre avoient destruitz et abatuz enterre.

(fo. 271)

ever, giving to the aforesaid king of England and to his heirs the town of Berwick with the county. This same year on the fifth day before the nones of December[42] pope John XXII died at Avignon and on Sunday was buried in the great church near the palace. Be it known that at the same time that the said sir Edward Balliol paid his homage, earl Patrick paid his own homage to the king of England, [swearing] to be faithful and loyal to him and to his heirs for ever, to hold of him and of his heirs his land which he had in the realm of Scotland, and to do what he promised to the king of England, [that is] to make all the lords of Scotland obedient and subject to him and to sir Edward Balliol who was king of Scotland. And for this the king of England gave him a great amount of treasure, that is to say 1,000 pounds, to put right and repair his manors and his towns which the English had destroyed and razed to the ground.

---

[42] There is no 5 *Non. Dec.*: that would be in fact *Kal. Dec.*, i.e. 1 December. Pope John XXII died on 4 December, i.e. *pridie Non. Dec.*, and in 1334 not the given 1333.

Index

The index includes all major variations on personal names, but minor variations of letters have not been noted.

Yorkshire Archaeological Society
Record Series

Attention is drawn to the fact that the *Record Series* volumes listed below are still available. Subscribers are entitled to a substantial discount. Some of these volumes are in very short supply. Orders should be sent to The Librarian, Yorkshire Archaeological Society, Claremont, 23 Clarendon Road, Leeds LS2 9NZ.

Vol.	Year	
11, 14, 19, 22, 24, 26, 28, 32, 35	1891–1905	Index to Wills in York Registry: 1514–1636
23, 31, 37	1897–1906	Yorkshire Inquisitions: pts 2–4, 1283–1309
40	1909	Paver's Marriage Licences: pt. 1: 1630–1645
41	1909	Yorkshire Star Chamber Proceedings: pt. 1
44	1911	Yorkshire Assize Rolls, John & Henry III
126	1960	Survey of Settrington, 1600
128	1965	Letters of James Tate
129	1966	Fasti Parochiales: pt. III; Deanery of Dickering
131 & 137	1968–75	Court Rolls of the Manor of Acomb: pts. 1 & 2
132	1969	Bolton Priory Rentals and Ministers Accounts, 1473–1539
133	1970	Fasti Parochiales: pt. IV; Deanery of Craven
134	1972	Yorkshire Probate Inventories, 1542–1689
136	1974	Constable of Everingham Estate Correspondence
138	1976	York Civic Records, vol. IX
139	1977/8	Leeds Friends' Minute Book, 1692–1712
140	1979/80	The Fountains Abbey Lease Book
141	1981	Selected Rentals and Accounts of Medieval Hull, 1293–1528
142	1982	The Diary of Charles Fothergill, 1805
143	1983	Fasti Parochiales: pt. V; Deanery of Buckrose
144	1984	The Customs Accounts of Hull, 1453–1490
145	1985	Early Tudor Craven
146	1986	The Archdeaconry of Richmond in the Eighteenth Century

The Society has one or two copies only of the following volumes: 94–110, 117–122, 125, 127.

For EU product safety concerns, contact us at Calle de José Abascal, 56–1°, 28003 Madrid, Spain or eugpsr@cambridge.org.

www.ingramcontent.com/pod-product-compliance
Ingram Content Group UK Ltd.
Pitfield, Milton Keynes, MK11 3LW, UK
UKHW012345130625
459647UK00009B/556